RUNNING WILD

A QUEST FOR HEALING ACROSS 7 CONTINENTS

BOBBY O'DONNELL

www.mascotbooks.com

Running Wild: A Quest for Healing Across 7 Continents

©2020 Bobby O'Donnell. All Rights Reserved. No part of this publication may be reproduced, stored in a retrieval system or transmitted in any form by any means electronic, mechanical, or photocopying, recording or otherwise without the permission of the author.

Visit www.runningwildbook.com to see photos from all the adventures told in the book, to contact the author, or to arrange speaking engagements.

All dates and locations at the beginning of each chapter are in reference to where the marathon took place, not where the chapter begins. Some names in this book have been changed to protect privacy. All events described are from the personal perspective and memory of the author unless otherwise noted.

Cover Photo: Joe Mann-Foinaven, Northwest Scotland

For more information, please contact:
Mascot Books
620 Herndon Parkway #320
Herndon, VA 20170
info@mascotbooks.com

Library of Congress Control Number: 2019915692

CPSIA Code: PRFRE1219A
ISBN-13: 978-1-64543-101-5

Printed in Canada

In loving memory of Rachel Collar.

For my mom and dad. Without their endless
support, love, and encouragement, my
dreams would remain just that: dreams.

CONTENTS

NOTE FROM THE AUTHOR

Why? When I describe my adventures to others, that is the question I hear the most. Those adventures have often been physically challenging, emotionally painful, and very expensive, so the question is certainly a logical one. To be truthful, I've found it difficult to conceive an explanation that makes sense to most people. I tend to revert to the famous words of Sir Edmund Hilary, "because it's there," but my family and close friends know the anguish and tragedy that really motivated me to run around the globe. I will attempt to share that here as authentically as I can, my triumphs and successes just as much as my mistakes and poor judgment.

In the end, I hope to demonstrate that it really is possible to continue reaching for your dreams, even when the last glimmer of hope seems to have vanished. With willpower and commitment, it is possible to change the path of your life at any moment. Sometimes life sucks, and the world seems to be conspiring against you, but you still have the power to change the trajectory of your existence.

In my case, it was my survival of the Boston Marathon bombing and the death of a close friend that inspired me to reevaluate my life from top to bottom. Little did I know that the soul-searching would give birth to my global adventure, one beyond my wildest dreams. No matter what your own challenges might be, I am living proof that you can have that kind of adventure too.

CHAPTER ONE

THE WORST DAY OF MY LIFE

Boston, Massachusetts
April 2013

Boom. The terrible, percussive sound of the first explosion drowned out every other noise in Boston, both literally and figuratively. The horror of that sound on a sunny Monday afternoon, April 15, 2013, was just the start of the chaos. *Boom.* Twelve seconds later came another. Bewildered and terrified, I stood near the finish line of the Boston Marathon on Massachusetts Avenue, stopped by police officers who seemed equally perplexed. Then thousands of screaming spectators came running towards me from the direction of the finish line.

My body trembled like never before in my nineteen years on the planet. It was consumed and nearly paralyzed by fear, my mind screaming with white noise. Then, in those early seconds, the sickening thought came to me for the first time: *My family.* Every person who I loved and cared about was waiting for me at the finish line, close to where those horrific blasts seemed to have originated. I felt a devastating certainty. My family was dead. They had supported my somewhat crazy desire to run and finish the Boston Marathon and would be there to see it to the end. They were at the finish line, directly in harm's way, because of me.

• • •

The chain of events that led me to that moment on the streets of Boston began many years prior. Running had no part of what was a fairly typical and uneventful childhood. However; whether you were a runner or not, the Boston Marathon is one of the most celebrated days of the year in my home state of Massachusetts, always falling on the third Monday of April and the state holiday of Patriots' Day.

Growing up near Boston, I had always been aware of the growing excitement in the city at the start of April each year. The sun began to shine brighter after a long harsh winter, the days grew longer, and spring would finally begin to reveal itself in the warming temperatures and budding trees. The Boston Marathon, the oldest continuously run marathon in the world, was as much a part of the northeastern spring as any of those things.

The famed race is celebrated by families, runners, college students, beer drinkers, wine sippers, and sports fans in every raucous combination. Parties and cookouts foreshadowed the summer to come. Everyone knew someone who was running in the marathon, whether it was a family member, the mailman, or the overly boastful guy from the gym, almost every person in New England had some connection to the event. At one point or another many New Englanders will resolve to run Boston themselves. Although few ever do, each year thousands have the motivation, perseverance, and often a dash of luck that leads them to the 26.2-mile route through eight Massachusetts towns to finish on Boylston Street in the heart of Boston, in front of thousands of screaming supporters.

Growing up, I toyed with this same ambition. In eighth grade I even wrote it in bold letters on my bucket list, along with diving the Great Barrier Reef and attending the Super Bowl. I had no clue as to the training and commitment that was necessary, and I never had any serious intentions on following through until my junior year in high school.

I had dabbled in several sports growing up, but running never really interested me. Little did I know that running would become one of the great passions of my life, changing it in ways I could never have dreamed of, and teaching me life lessons I never otherwise would have learned. I distinctly remember the day my passion was born.

● ● ●

Each year, my family celebrates my father's birthday, April 21st, by taking a commuter boat into Boston for an enjoyable day in the city. The day he turned fifty-five, we were walking down a street in the North End when I noticed something unusual. Everywhere I looked there were lean and fit men and women, limping down the street wearing bright smiles, all dressed in incredibly sharp-looking Adidas windbreakers; a slick black base with vibrant green stripes on the sleeves and a reflective silver logo on the back. On the collar was "26.2." I told my dad I was going to get one of those jackets one day.

"You're going to run the marathon?" he asked jokingly.

He knew that at the time I had never run a 5K, so his skeptical laughter was more than justified.

"Yeah Dad, I'm running Boston." It may not have been a new dream, but this time there was a sense of conviction, and I had every intention of following through.

The next step was to determine if I actually enjoyed running. That seemed to be a pretty important prerequisite for participation in one of the world's oldest and most popular marathons. The next weekend at the local running store, I tried on several pairs of shoes before settling on a sleek pair of neon Nike sneakers adorned with a cobalt blue swoosh on the sides.

My first official run was a two-mile jaunt down Elm Street in Easton—a beautifully quaint road in my hometown that was slightly downhill at the start and gradually uphill at the finish. Beforehand I had envisioned myself doubled over in pain at the end of my first run, puking into an overpriced rose bush. But I didn't die. I tapped the hood of my car at the end of the run. I didn't own a runner's watch. My phone said it had taken me just less than twenty minutes.

Next, I needed to commit to a smaller race, which would provide me with a short-term goal and help with motivation for my training. One of the most popular in Massachusetts (aside from the marathon) was a seven-mile event on Cape Cod called the Falmouth Road Race, a beautiful seaside route that attracts more than ten thousand runners each year, with an elite field. Many of the entrants are selected by lottery.

I submitted my application on Cinco de Mayo of 2011, still having no real idea of the challenges of distance running. Two weeks later I was accepted. What if I hadn't been? Would that have ended my running career before it even began? As a child I would find myself rolling my eyes at my mom's favorite mantra: "Things happen for a reason." Yet the older I get, the more truth I find in this sentiment. Coincidences may be just that, but I increasingly feel the presence of fate amongst these apparently random happenings. Paraphrasing Paulo Coelho, the Brazilian author responsible for my favorite book, *The Alchemist*, if something is supposed to happen, the whole universe will conspire to make it so.

I had a few months to train and spent the summer slowly increasing my endurance; building muscles I did not know I had. It was not enjoyable at first, not one bit. My first attempt to complete seven miles was a hot and humid day in July, about a month before the event. Sweat poured down my face and stung my eyes. I pounded along, aggressively willing my legs to keep going while I fought the unpleasantness. Feeling frustrated and defeated, I quit after five miles, calling my mom to pick me up.

That day I questioned my goals and motives. *I'm not a runner. What am I trying to do here*? But quitting wasn't really an option. I had stated my commitment to family and friends, knowing that once I had done this, I was the sort of person who would keep to it. Those hard, early days of training actually led me to discover a deeper motivation to run. Initially just wanting to get around and tick off the miles, I soon found myself truly striving to better myself, to not just finish the race, but also to conquer it.

A month later, my parents dropped me off at the starting line of the Falmouth Road Race. I listened to the conversations around me—moms walking the distance in under two hours, seasoned marathoners shooting for a personal best. The positive energy at the starting line was unlike anything I had experienced. Runners truly are a rare breed of people, a good example of the true enthusiasm and community found amongst people who have discovered a real passion. They have so much love for what they do and care deeply for their fellow competitors.

A tan, toned, fit man in his forties with shaved legs and intimidating sunglasses walked up to me and patted my shoulder. I'm sure he could tell I was nervous in my first experience with pre-race jitters.

"You ready man!?" he yelled over the pumping music, with a laid-back California-like tone.

"Yep!" I shouted back, trying to camouflage my nerves. "This is my first race."

"What!? No way! Really! Oh man, you're gonna love it! I've done all kinds of marathons and this is still one of my all-time favorite races!"

He gave me typical advice: don't go out too fast; make sure to drink at every water stop; listen to your body; and so on and so forth. But then, he told me something no one had before. "When you see that finish line, and you hear the crowd yelling, and you see your family cheering for you, close your eyes for a second. Think about all the hard work it took to get to this one day, this one moment. Be proud of yourself for having the balls to commit all your time to it. Soak that in and remember it and you will always be inspired for your next race. You'll get to your marathon."

It turns out he was a coach, one who had trained many people to run marathons. His parting wisdom was that anyone could run a marathon with the right training, dedication, and iron in their heart.

The starting countdown blared over the loudspeakers. Then, I ran. The race went by in a flash. I finished in less than an hour and loved every second of it. The experience was everything that kindly coach said it would be and more—my family cheering, the fans screaming, the music thumping the whole way. I couldn't have been more thrilled had I been walking up to bat at Fenway Park. I was hooked. No matter what it took, I was going to run my marathon, and for the first time I truly believed it.

I signed up for my first marathon that very night. A Google search revealed that the Philadelphia Marathon would take place exactly one hundred days from then, just enough time, in my mind, to train for that intimidating distance.

At seventeen, I didn't realize the distance between Boston and Philadelphia. When I told my mom about my impulse decision, and the race that was just thirteen weeks away, I made it sound like it would be a quick drive down the road. The look on her face told me differently, but she promised me she would figure out how to get us there if I could do my part; actually train for my first marathon.

Google delivered me to Hal Higdon's training plan for beginners. It became my Bible for the next few months.

I soon experienced my first long run, my first blister, my first running app, and the end of my experiment with five-toed shoes. There were times when I felt like I was kidding myself, foolish for attempting a marathon with no running experience to speak of, but I had made a commitment—not to mention the $150 registration fee, which Dad lent me the money for. Importantly, at this early stage I seemed to sense that the Philadelphia Marathon was just the first step in a much longer journey.

After weeks of training, two half-marathons in New England, and a twenty-mile run, all of which I barely survived, I boarded a flight to Philadelphia with my parents and grandmother in tow. From our hotel, we made the short walk to my first marathon expo; none of us had a clue what to expect. I was overwhelmed the moment we walked through the door, confronted with the wall-to-wall throngs of experienced marathoners, all feeding off the buzz of anticipation that hummed through the event center.

I proudly marched past the half-marathon check-in to the bright-eyed and energetic volunteers at the full marathon tables. We were given my marathon bib, then meandered amongst the endless booths, each of which were pushing different brands of multicolored running kits, energy supplements, insoles and race apparel. After a quick pit stop at a street vendor, where my dad bought an, "authentic" Philly cheesesteak, we were back at our hotel, still buzzing from the energy of the other marathoners.

My family coaxed me through the nervousness that only intensified on race morning. The next time I saw them was out on the course, with big smiles and even bigger signs cheering me on. By mile twenty-one, it dawned on me that this was the furthest I had ever run. *Holy shit. I'm actually going to run a marathon.* Until that moment, I had not really thought of *finishing* a marathon.

My pace increased. In less than an hour, I would be a member of that group that I so much admired, a "marathoner."

Then it happened. I hit "the wall" for the first time, and it was every bit as awful as I had heard. My body seemed frozen, no matter how much I willed it forward. I started walking—or more accurately limping—on the side of the road. Any forward progress was a victory at that point. My muscles cramped, ached, and burned. I wanted to curl into a ball on the pavement and have someone roll me to the finish line. "The wall" is a heartless bitch.

I made a deal with myself: run two minutes then I could walk for three. I was slowly covering ground in this fashion when I reached the marker for mile twenty-six and a switch, somewhere, was flipped. It was as if my old legs had been replaced with a brand new pair; fresh and full of energy. I kicked these foreign legs forward, faster and faster, at a pace unfamiliar to me.

I crossed the finish line of my first marathon, hands above my head in triumph. That finish line would be the first of many in a journey that would take me to some of the most remote places on this planet, but that day, that feeling at the finish line was all I knew. It was bliss. To work so hard for that one day and experience that moment of achievement in the face of all the odds and all the self-doubt, it was fulfilling beyond words. All of those cold runs in the rain, early morning wake-ups, and blistered feet made this moment worth everything. The dedication and commitment was what made the feeling at that finish line so sweet.

After a shower at the hotel, I knew there was something I needed to do right away. I sat on my bed, opened up my MacBook, and tried to find the Boston Marathon sign-up page. It wasn't there. The marathon website was, but no sign-up page. Then my heart sank when I read the qualifying standards: *Men 18–34, 3:05:00*. Impossible. There was no way in hell I could do that. That was fifty-three minutes—almost an hour—faster than the time I had just run.

Back in Boston, the marathon became an obsession. I learned the history, the route, elevation profile, past winners, entry fees, and a whole lot about some guy named Bill Rodgers. I searched high and low for a loophole around the qualifying time, a way to get in, without running a sub-seven marathon pace.

Aside from really whipping my ass into shape, the only other option would be to run by raising money for a charity. This immediately appealed to me, but how would a seventeen-year-old kid raise the minimum requirement of $5,000 for a bib number? By November, all charity applications for the Boston Marathon of 2012 had closed anyway. Greatly discouraged, I hung up my running shoes for a couple of months.

The unusually warm spring in New England inspired me to sign up for a half-marathon in Rhode Island. I ran a couple more 5K races over the summer, but nothing serious. What did happen was that I started to realize I was running simply for the pleasure and beauty of it. Up on the trails in New Hampshire, around the lakes and through the mountains, I began to forge a bond with the land that I had never had before. Each run in the woods left me craving more; to count the trees, smell the pines, and feel the fresh breeze across my face. The more I ran, the more in tune I became with everything around me, each individual aspect of the environment, and the beauty of nature as a whole. That summer I felt more human, more a part of this world, than ever before.

The summer quickly passed and in the autumn I was off to start my first year away from home at Saint Anselm College. Right before school began, I received an email from the Boston Athletic Association (BAA), which said that the charity application process for the 2013 Boston Marathon had opened. Instead of spending my first weekend in college at the library or hanging out with new friends, I occupied my time filling out applications to charities I'd like to support, justifying why I deserved to be considered for one of those iconic Boston Marathon bibs.

Later that October, I received one of my greatest gifts: an entry to the 2013 Boston Marathon. I will forever be grateful to those who helped me get my number, and most importantly my Uncle Sean. Now, I had the opportunity to raise money and run for a charity of my choice. That decision was easy: Boston Children's Hospital.

● ● ●

My desire to work in medicine began on July 16, 2009, a sunny Thursday afternoon in Meredith, New Hampshire. I was fifteen and had recently finished my freshman year of high school visiting Lake Winnipesaukee with my friends. We were ecstatic with the freedom of the summer ahead, kicking it off with an amazing day on the water.

My father had brought us down to the lake, just a short walk from the house where we stayed. We tossed the Frisbee, played wiffle ball, and enjoyed the pure joy of being kids in the outdoors—no real responsibilities yet weighing on our adolescent minds.

John Lee was, and still is, one of my best friends—he had grown up in South Korea and immigrated to the United States only a few years prior. Many young Koreans do not learn to swim as children, but John had spent the previous few days swimming in a life jacket from my dad's boat and had grown more comfortable in the water. So on this day when a Frisbee landed in the lake, John went out to retrieve it.

I was sitting a hundred meters away, with the cooler full of water and soda, when my entire life changed. One of my friends came sprinting up towards me, his panicked shouts wrenching my gut from my body.

"Bobby! John went in the water...and he didn't come back out!" he screamed.

I felt the blood drain from my face.

"What?!"

"He swam out to get a Frisbee and then we realized that he never came back in!"

I sprinted back down the path. On the beach, the other boys were frantic.

"Call my dad! Call 911!" I yelled as I sprinted into the water and swam towards the Frisbee floating fifty feet away.

I dove below the water when I neared the Frisbee. Silt and debris impaired my vision, my hands finding the bottom at about ten feet. I swiveled my head wildly as I searched for any sign of my best friend. Oxygen-deprived, my lungs burned as I fought against my instincts which tried to drag me towards the surface. But then I thought I saw a glint of white. I kicked back to the surface to gulp a quick breath and immediately dove again, seeing John's limp body coming into view, the green of the lake casting a haunting shadow over him. His hair flowed with the pulse of the water. His eyes were closed, his mouth open, his limbs limp and lifeless. The sight of him would be the focus of my nightmares for years to come.

Another friend who swam out with me helped lift John to the surface. I remember the glare of the sun as I wrapped my arms under Johns, kicking and stroking with all of my energy to get my friend back to the shore. When my feet touched bottom, I dragged him by the arms to dry ground. John's lips were blue; his eyes rolled back into his head. He wasn't breathing and had no pulse. I began chest compressions and completed a two-minute cycle of CPR when my father arrived. He had decades of experience as an emergency room nurse and firefighter-para-medic and though his presence should have been calming, my world was shattering around me. Nonetheless, he administered rescue breaths while I continued chest compressions.

We estimated that John had been in the water for seven minutes. I yelled at him, screaming at my friend to come back. With every second that he was unresponsive, our hope dwindled. It began to seem as if hours had passed since we pulled him from the lake. Tears burned down my cheeks as I choked back muffled cries at the thought of my best friend being gone forever. But then, after fifteen minutes of CPR, John spit up a gulp of water into my father's face.

He was awake and alert by the time the ambulance arrived, speaking to us with no neurological impairment. Doctors later attributed John's improbable survival to the hypothermic state induced by the cold water, which preserved his brain function.

That day deepened my bond with my best friend and I felt beyond lucky to still have him in my life. We even held the potentially awkward accolade of being each other's first kiss, to the absolute hilarity of all our friends. The traumatic events of our trip to the lake also inspired my choice of career—emergency medicine. I could not imagine a more rewarding profession than having the chance to make a difference in people's lives on a daily basis. By my eighteenth birthday and end of my senior year in high school, I was a certified EMT with plans to study pre-med, and eventually become an emergency room doctor.

It was through these early experiences in medicine that my awe for Boston Children's Hospital began. I recognized right away that handling pediatric emergencies were some of the most challenging and heart-wrenching aspects of working in this field. In those early days of my emergency medical career, I was terrified by pediatric calls. We anticipate the possibility of seeing death on every shift, but not with children.

The fact will always remain that too many children around the world are involved in acute accidents or affected by horrific diseases—some terminal—every year. However, there will also always be heroic people and institutions that do what they can to try and prevent that. Boston Children's Hospital is one of the best in the world. Through a good friend, Matt Howley, who worked for the Critical Care Transport team at Children's, I had the opportunity to volunteer there. I witnessed firsthand how this elite group of paramedics, nurses, and physicians transferred critically ill pediatric patients to Boston from around the world for treatment. It is hard to comprehend the stress involved in caring for desperately sick or injured children in the back of an ambulance or airplane, keeping them stable until arrival at the hospital. During my tour of the hospital, I had the chance to meet patients being treated in various units. I anticipated a silence on those hospital floors as families and staff awaited grim news. The reality was anything but.

Terminally ill children played in their rooms, smiling and laughing with their families, nurses, and doctors. These kids had every reason to be bitter for the poor hand they had been dealt. Instead, they seemed able to cherish life, grateful for the time to play, and laugh, and smile.

The kindness, dedication, and altruism of the staff on that campus, from the janitors to the chief physicians and CEO, make it a truly magical place. Nurses and doctors there have some of the most difficult jobs in the world, and not one I believe I could do day after day. It was for this reason I wanted to make a contribution in a different way, and why I chose Children's Hospital as my Boston Marathon charity.

I could not have had a more profound motivation to train and fundraise than those children and the people who care for them. My running was no longer about a marathon jacket. It was about something much more meaningful.

Training for the Boston Marathon began four months before the big race, in December 2012. I bought my first pair of running tights, not knowing whether I should feel embarrassed or like a super hero. I ran on Christmas morning in a Santa hat, on hour-long breaks between college classes, and managed to put in long runs on Sunday before the Patriot's kickoff. I ran during snowstorms strong enough to cancel classes, and on days cold enough that my icicle-covered beard tickled my nose by the time I was finished.

The finish line of the Boston Marathon was the last thing I thought about before falling asleep at night, and the first thing when I woke up in the morning. A "Countdown to Marathon Monday" poster hung on the wall above my dorm room bed. The marathon logo was the screensaver on my phone.

I founded an organization called "26.2 for Children" to spearhead my fundraising. Social media was the primary means to get the word out, but local news outlets began to pick up my story; promoting a charitable golf tournament I would host the week before the Boston Marathon. It was stressful, a nineteen-year-old college kid trying to raise $5,000, but my experience at Children's Hospital was never far from my mind. I was resolved to do whatever it took to raise money for them, and promised each donor that for their contribution, I would cross that finish line on

April 15th. People could not have been more generous. By the second week of April 2013, after the first annual 26.2 for Children Golf Tournament, we had raised $7,589.

I was speechless. My family and friends had joined with complete strangers to far surpass my fundraising goal for Children's Hospital Boston. I felt like we were helping to make a difference for something truly important. There may have been countless who raised more, but I could not have been prouder.

By the Sunday evening of April 14th, the fundraising behind me, I could sit on my bed and reflect on the momentous day to come. After all the dreams, planning, and training, the moment of the Boston Marathon had finally arrived. At no other time in my life had I felt such excitement, such a feeling of anticipation. After hours of staring at the ceiling of my childhood bedroom, I drifted off to sleep.

I was wide awake from the moment I opened my eyes six hours later—no morning grogginess plagued me that day. My father was waiting downstairs to drive me to the finish area on Boylston Street. From there I would board the bus to the start line in the town of Hopkinton.

My breakfast was a banana and energy bar, quickly choked down as I paced the floor, unable to settle. I double-checked my gear bag, slid on my running clothes and windbreaker, and joined my dad in the car. By the end of this day I knew I would return wearing a Boston Marathon finisher jacket.

I will never forget how still and empty the city seemed that morning. I found comfort in this, knowing that in just a few hours, millions of people would be lining the streets. Cheering with equal passion for the world's finest distance runners and for amateurs alike, all of us participating in one of Boston's most important and longest traditions.

The city finally seemed to come alive as we drove into the heart of Boston, approaching Boylston Street. Police cars and shuttle buses lined the roadways. Volunteers and runners scuttled from tent to tent carrying large cardboard boxes and the bright yellow gear check bags.

This was it. I gave my dad a big hug.

"I love you," he said. "See you at the finish line!"

I found a window seat on the school-bus-turned-shuttle that would drive us 26.2 miles out of the city to Hopkinton. A middle-aged man from Canada sat down next to me, but we pretty much kept our thoughts to ourselves.

Closer to Hopkinton, signs welcoming runners were everywhere. I finally confessed to the man next to me that this would be my first Boston Marathon. He smiled and told me that it was going to be the best day of my life. Given the trembling of excitement that rippled through my body, I certainly believed him.

Raw emotion washed over my body as the race began, thousands of runners moving as one around me, all running for charity. Each stride brought me closer to what I had been dreaming of for years. Looking around me I didn't see the most fit, or fastest runners in the race, but I saw some of the most passionate. Shirts were decorated with pictures of cancer survivors, children's signatures, and memorial ribbons. We all shared a purpose larger than the race; a drive to reach the finish line that was motivated by things more important than our own personal goals. I felt part of a team, an army of ordinary people attempting to do something extraordinary to make the world a better place.

The crowd screamed through those first dozen miles, which was a blur of emotion and water stops. My name was written on pink duct tape that stretched beneath my race number and strangers cheered me on, pushing me ever closer towards the city of Boston.

I knew by mile five that I had started too fast, but I kept pushing the pace, fueled by the crowd and the downhill parts of the course at the beginning. I would soon pay for it and the pain truly began at mile eighteen. My ambitious pace had provoked a hip flexor injury that I had been nursing for the past few weeks. Water stops became "walking stops" so I could try to ease the pain and rest my weary legs. I slurped down every soggy paper cup of water that volunteers passed into my shaking hands. Finishing in less than four hours was still possible but seemed less and less likely. My goal was to get from water stop to water stop and continue to grind it out through the pain.

The cheering of students from Boston College, the loudest of the race in my opinion, gave me a much-needed jolt of energy at mile twenty-one. I ran to the side and picked my pace up to something much faster than I should have, but my legs did not protest, they let the excitement in my brain run free. Hands reached out and I slapped them all as I ran by, until one of those hands held a shiny blue can of Bud Light.

Without thinking, my hand grabbed the sweaty blue aluminum that glistened in the sunlight and I ripped the tab, foam spraying into the air. The crowd roared while I brought the overflowing can of piss-warm beer to my mouth, and slammed down a load of carbs.

My spirits lifted instantly and a short time later, one of my best friends from college, Brian Higgins, came up beside me to accompany me over the last few miles. My mind and body were failing, but Brian, who is also a talented comedian, did his best to distract me from my pain with humor.

"How are you feeling, dude?"

"Like shit," I muttered.

"You're about to finish the Boston Marathon, only a couple miles man, you got this!"

Brian smiled through his beard and patted my back. It sank in that he was right. I was only a few miles from finishing the Boston Marathon.

I teared up, reflecting on what had brought me to this moment— every single run, building to this finish line. All of the fundraising, volunteering, and events were all for today. My friends, family, and colleagues had all invested and believed in me, supporting me financially and emotionally. I had never felt more loved. What had started as a silly quest to earn a flashy jacket had become a way of life, introducing me to a passion that I never would have otherwise discovered. I felt that all of my time and effort had been repaid tenfold.

At mile twenty-five the crowds grew louder and larger, people stacked five-deep on the barricades, willing the runners on to the finish line. The Massachusetts Avenue Bridge finally came into view, and I knew I would shortly be making that famous right turn onto Hereford Street.

Boom.

I didn't think much of the loud crash at first. But then, as I made my way up the Mass Ave Bridge, runners in front of me began to slow. When another monstrous noise echoed twelve seconds after the first, we all began to sense that there was something seriously wrong. Police officers began to stop runners as they turned onto Hereford Street. My first thought was a car accident. All around me runners looked confused, asking questions to police while jogging in place, knowing that the finish line was so close. Police told us to be patient, that something in front of us was "being taken care of." The truth was, those police officers had no idea what was halting forward progress either, they could not have begun to imagine the chaos and destruction just ahead.

People were becoming irritated. *I* was becoming irritated. I was 0.6 miles from the finish line. No one just stops the Boston Marathon. A car accident wasn't possible, for it was a closed course. What the hell was going on?

Then the police told us that the race was over because of an incident. We were shocked, confused, and angry, not knowing of the horrors that had occurred just out of our view. The first inkling of the enormity of what had happened came when spectators who had been at the finish line began running in our direction, as if to escape from something.

At this point I had been running for four hours. I was cold, tired, and trying to comprehend what was happening, that everything I had dreamed of and worked so hard for had been abruptly terminated in such a nightmarish way. Brian's shoulder supported my shaky body as my legs trembled beneath me, jarred from the abrupt stop after hours of continuous motion.

Brian and I looked at each other, searching for answers, but found only fear and confusion. I finally stopped one spectator who was running by me, asking her what had happened up there. I'll never forget the look of terror in her eyes as she told me that bombs had exploded in the grandstands at the finish line.

That was where my family was waiting for me, every single person that I loved. The whole world around me began to shatter. Each word that came from that woman's mouth was like a brick being tossed through a glass window. Her panic and terror were too real, too raw for her story to be anything other than the truth. My priority became locating my family, whether they were alive or not. Brian was in the city with a group of people from our college cross-country team, many of whom were behind us, not ahead. Neither of us had ever been victimized by a terrorist attack and as teenagers were not prepared to handle the stress of decision-making under such duress. In that moment, we split up to head in the directions we needed to. While Brian went back to find our teammates, I made my way to the finish line.

I limped to the nearest police officer, telling him I was a trained EMT, begging him to allow me to help. He, too, looked terrified.

"Son, you just focus on walking, and get the hell away from here," he said.

I had no idea what to do. I had never seen a police officer with his weapon drawn, never mind with such a look of confusion and anguish impressed upon his face. What should I do? Where should I go? I certainly wasn't carrying a cell phone during the race, so I had no way to try and reach my family. I attempted to slow down my spinning mind and develop a plan. I finally approached one of the many members of the media that had instantly converged on the area and pleaded to borrow a phone. A reporter handed me his. I dialed my mother's number. I listened to a recording that informed me the call could not be completed.

I received the same result when I tried my father, grandmother, aunt, cousin, and mother again. I despised that prerecorded voice.

It was with sick certainty that I concluded the reason my calls didn't go through was because my family was dead; the family who had come together in Boston because of me. I started wandering in a daze, in no particular direction, already wondering how I would live the rest of my life, when I had brought such devastation on the people I love.

I noticed people emerging from their apartments with food, water, jackets, and clothes for the cold, tired, and distraught runners. These were the first gestures of a wave of kindnesses from the people of Boston. The majority of runners were from all over the country and around the world, without knowledge of the city, their phones, or wallets, and Bostonians took them in. One of them, a woman, gave me some water and invited me to sit on her steps while I listened to an endless stream of sirens. I felt weak and sick to my stomach. I borrowed another cell phone. I started to weep after I got another recording, tasting the salt from my dried sweat. Hours had passed since the bombing.

I finally left my place on those steps and approached another reporter, borrowing his phone. If calls weren't going through, maybe a text would.

It's Bobby. Where are you? Are you okay?

Though it felt like an eternity, the phone buzzed within minutes. I stared at the screen, lightheaded with relief.

Oh my God. Meet us outside of Yawkey Way near Fenway. We are okay.

I broke down and hugged the reporter whose phone had delivered the greatest news of my life. The weariness in my legs was gone. I sprinted towards Fenway Park.

I later learned that the bombs had exploded across from the grandstands, which is why my family had escaped physically unscathed. Had my Uncle Sean not given my family VIP passes for the grandstands, they would have been where the bombs had exploded

My father had been receiving text alerts of my progress and, anticipating my approach, was taking a cell phone video when he captured bomb number one. Again, fate seemed to intervene on our behalf. Were it not for my hip injury, I would have been near the blast zone myself when the explosions occurred, taking their deadly toll.

Rounding the corner of another old brick building, I saw the blond hair of my mother walking hurriedly with my family in tow amongst a sea of panicked people. We locked eyes and she wept as we rushed towards each other and engaged in a tight embrace. I could feel her tears mixing with the sweat that had dried onto the collar of my running shirt. Never before in my life had I engaged in a hug so meaningful—one I had no idea I would get to experience again.

Glancing at the rest of my family, I could see the relief on their faces, but also something different. There was an unspoken change in their expression; I could see the memory of horror in their eyes; eyes that had just bore witness to carnage typically reserved for soldiers at war. Although inexplicably grateful to have my family back, I quickly realized that our lives had changed forever.

I made my way through each person and hugged them, cried, and held them tight. My heart sank when I saw that my father was not with them.

As it turns out, my dad was a hero that day. When the explosions went off, he ran towards them and hopped over the race barrier. He then found himself staring down the barrel of a police officer's gun at a time when the authorities were struggling to distinguish between good guys and bad. My dad identified himself as a firefighter-paramedic and the police officer lowered his gun and told him to "go to work."

My dad became one of the first responders, rummaging through the rubble, fixing tourniquets, and applying pressure to control bleeding. He assumed a command role, directing bystanders who could assist with the injured and organizing their movement into waiting ambulances. My father received a number of awards for his heroics that day, and no one was prouder of him than me.

We left the city without him; he was still busy taking care of the sick and dying. The drive from the city was quiet and somber. My relief at the survival of my family and me was short-lived, soon replaced by fear and guilt. Why should I have been so lucky when others had not? I had no idea of the extent to which that guilt and those questions would haunt me in the coming weeks, months, and years. The trauma of those hours spent believing my loved ones no longer existed would take a heavy toll. That day changed me, as it did so many others. What I thought was going to be the best day of my life would now forever be remembered as one of my worst.

CHAPTER TWO

BROKEN

Boston, Massachusetts
April 2014

Within a day or two of the bombing, you couldn't walk a block in Massachusetts without seeing "Boston Strong" on a hat, t-shirt, or bumper sticker. For weeks, local news outlets filled papers and television screens with stories of the terrorists, the heroism of everyday people or miraculous recoveries. Boston Strong became a phrase of unity and defiance adopted across the nation. I was initially swept up in the emotion and patriotism of the time, but soon found that I needed those after effects to end. I needed the world to move on, to have a day when there was just one hour where I didn't think about what happened on April 15, 2013. I needed to heal.

It would be a long, long time before that day would come.

Because I had survived, I didn't feel I had the right to sadness or depression. Instead, I was consumed with anger that such a terrible attack had been carried out on one of Boston's most festive days of the year. How could I feel sorry for myself when so many other people had lost so much? My heart still pumped blood. I could walk. There were no funerals for me to attend.

My anger and frustration only intensified when the nightmares began weeks later. Again, I didn't feel entitled to the trauma and pain, but the terrors that plagued my sleep were incessant and I couldn't will them away as much as I tried. There were horrible nights when in my sleep I would see the bloody and broken bodies of the ones I loved amid the twisted metal on Boylston Street; a broken cell phone in my hand; the constant horror that it was my fault they were there in the first place. Night after night I would awaken tangled in my sheets, drenched in sweat. Why had these images implanted themselves so firmly in my unconscious? My family were among the lucky ones.

So the nightmares became my secret. I feared being scoffed at. My repressed emotions weighed heavier every day and began to infiltrate my waking moments too. Large crowds made me nervous. I couldn't stand even the thought of returning to Boston. The sight of an unattended bag or backpack induced a cold sweat. Anytime my parents didn't answer a phone call, I had to fight back panic. Hatred for the bombers burned deep and monopolized my thoughts.

To add to the torment I realized I now despised running. The activity that had given me so much joy, my stress reliever after a hard day in the classroom, a way to be out in the beauty of nature, had been snatched away. Even the idea of lacing up my running shoes caused uneasiness in my stomach. It invited my brain to remember every detail of that April day: the screams, the sounds, the smells, the terror, the uncertainty of whether my family had survived. I never stopped running, but most days I felt numb when I did. Then there were the runs when numbness gave way to anger, pushing me to run faster and faster until my lungs burst, gulping for air, begging relief from the demons that closed in on me. I cried, yelled. A few times I collapsed and had to pull myself together for the run home. In some sadistic way, I needed to feel the pain running inspired. I didn't deserve to be sad, but I needed to suffer.

The Boston Marathon bombing ended lives, stole limbs, invaded dreams, and took away my passion.

I was a sophomore in college that fall, a busy time as I worked toward my undergraduate degree whilst being enrolled in paramedic school, and continuing to take shifts as an EMT. Even my work had become a trigger; each time we turned on the lights and blared the sirens of the ambulance on the way to an emergency, my mind was teleported back to the endless moans of the ambulances in the street the day of the bombing. There seemed to be nowhere I could go to escape; every part of my life was a reminder.

Somewhat counterintuitively, I looked to the next year's Boston Marathon in 2014 as a way to escape the darkness. If I could slog through the dreadful days of training, I could finish what had been stolen from me the year before, the chance to cross the finish line. So I kept up my miserable training routine through the winter.

Three months away from the race, the sense of constant anxiety increased. I was afraid that it would happen again, that I would put my family in danger and there would be nothing I could do about it. But as I remembered the helplessness and fear of that day the previous spring, the social pressure to run the race was building. This would be the year that we would "take back Boston." I didn't want to let anyone down by not running, but I was very unsure if I was emotionally able to bring myself to do so. At some points I even thought about faking an injury or fabricating another excuse for why I could not run.

A YouTube video I stumbled upon by chance changed this.

• • •

It was my father who began sending me TED Talks on YouTube, believing that the education they provided was almost the equivalent of what I was learning in the college classroom. I typically watched them on my lunch break between classes at Saint Anselm College. On a snowy mid-week day in February I was doing exactly this, sitting in the back of the lunch hall, occasionally glancing out into the ever-increasing whiteness outside. While watching a TED Talk Dad had sent me, something caught my eye in YouTube's "suggested tab." It was titled "Because I said I would," a talk by someone named Alex Sheen. I clicked the link, took a bite of yogurt, and was entranced immediately by the speaker's voice and stage presence. There was just something about him that drew me in.

I watched as Alex told his story, and the one of his organization, which is also titled "because I said I would." His father had died of lung cancer in September 2012 and Alex would go on to give the eulogy. As he thought about what he wanted to say, Alex knew that he wanted his father to be remembered for how he lived, not how he died. It was his father's commitment to keeping promises that Alex found most remarkable, and he felt the world would be a better place if more people lived in this way. Alex had an idea: the "promise card," which he presented during the tearful eulogy.

A simple concept, it was the size of a business card with "because I said I would," printed on the front bottom right corner and blank on the back. Alex conceived of people writing down their promises and giving them to whomever the promise was being made. When the promise was kept, the card would be handed back to the person who had made it. In the YouTube video, Alex cited studies that demonstrated promises written down were much more likely to be kept than those merely spoken. Accountability is the magic component.

In the lunch hall that day, I listened intently as Alex described his promise of sending ten cards anywhere in the world at no cost. His promises landed on the internet and soon went viral. Ten promise cards became nearly 10.3 million mailed to 153 different countries by the new nonprofit, *because I said I would*.

I emailed my dad the minute the talk ended. I was running the Boston Marathon in a few months. I had made a promise to my friends and family, Boston Children's Hospital, and to myself that I would finish the Boston Marathon and would hold myself personally accountable to fulfill my promise. In the back of my mind, I was also hoping that finishing the marathon would help bring a desperately needed peace to my life and allow me to heal.

I noticed big changes in my training. My mind was in a better place because I felt a renewed purpose. This race was no longer just about me, but about a network of people who had become involved in my marathon quest, I felt reconnected to that larger purpose that had been so important the first time around. Every time I laced my shoes up, it was another step closer to an achievement for my friends, family, and sick children in the hospital, their families and caregivers. I now felt more invested to do my part to "take back" the Boston Marathon. On the outside heel of my running shoes, I wrote, "because I said I would" in a black Sharpie.

Unfortunately, it would not be long until another slightly dramatic event would interrupt my progress before the big day in April. That March, I decided to take a trip with my mother and grandmother to Fort Myers, Florida, the spring training home of the Boston Red Sox. My grandmother, always Nana B to me, is a die-hard Red Sox fan. She would turn seventy-five in a few months and the trip and a preseason game would be an early present. Additionally, I was also looking forward to training runs without three layers of clothes protecting my body. The New England winter had been particularly brutal.

It was the first night of our vacation. Mom and Nana B shared a queen bed while I would sleep on a futon. When we were first getting settled, I moved it outside onto the balcony. It was paradise; each night

I would get to sleep with this beautiful view, the pool area below me and the crashing waves of the ocean just beyond that. Nighttime in Florida was comfortable enough outside to only be covered with a light blanket. Slowly, I drifted off, letting the sounds of the waves carry me into a deep slumber.

Sometime in the early morning, I was awakened by screams coming from the direction of the ocean as the sun began to rise on the horizon. My mom came to the sliding door.

"Did you hear that?" I asked.

"Yes," she said. "I thought you were falling off the balcony!"

In the dim light she looked frightened. Then, in the distance, we heard more screaming.

"Help! Help!"

I swung my legs out from under the covers of the futon. The cries were coming from the beach. I pulled on my shorts.

"What are you doing?" my mom asked.

"I need to go check that out."

"No, you don't, you need to stay put," she said. "You don't know what's happening."

But the shouts continued.

"Mom, I might be able to help this person," I said. "I'm going to see what it is at least."

"Robert Gerard O'Donnell, don't you dare go in that water!" she yelled as I rushed out the door, down the stairs, and sprinted through the lobby and past the pool. The shouts were getting louder. When I got to the beach, I saw a few other people, standing together by a dock, looking towards the source of the distressed cries. Darkness obscured whomever the desperate man or woman was, out in the water somewhere near the weather-beaten dock. Then we heard splashing. At a dock parallel to the one where we were standing, maybe fifty meters away, we saw a man in the water, clinging on to a rope that dangled from one of the docks.

We sprinted in that direction. The man in the water was elderly and fully clothed, flailing and splashing frantically in the water next to the dock, well out of reach below us.

I surprised myself by the calm that settled over me, attributing it to being in the midst of paramedic school, where I was frequently put through stressful, lifelike simulations. Only this time, it was real.

"There's no way we can lift him," I said. "We have to go in and get him."

We exchanged nervous glances at one another, and then set into action.

One man, who I would later learn was a doctor, immediately got on board. "I'll grab the pole from the pool net. You guys can use it as a guide to hold onto, and I'll help pull you in towards the beach."

A small woman with short, sandy brown hair and an athletic-looking young man identified themselves as strong swimmers. Others on the dock were trying to reassure the desperate man that help was coming, but his anxious shouts were now interrupted by the sound of gurgling water.

"Here's what we need to do," I said, addressing the two volunteers who would plunge into the dark ocean with me. "When we jump in, give me a shout so I know you're okay. It's still very dark. He's going to be moving around a lot until we get him calmed down, so make sure you don't get pulled under. I'll take the inside and you get under his right arm."

My mom appeared on the dock just as the three of us jumped into the water. The current was very strong, pulling us first under as we hit the water, then sucking us away from the elderly man out further to sea. It was clear why he was so reluctant to let go of the rope and try to grasp one of our hands.

I fought through the current to come up, wrapping my arms under his. The woman swam to his front.

"Sir, my name is Bobby and we're here to help you. Take some deep breaths. I need you to try and calm down."

He didn't reply, but his panicked shouting had ceased. The woman had jumped in with an inflatable pool tube that she was able to slide around him. The man seemed calmer but did not reply to my questions. My training kicked in. He looked exhausted. I also found myself wondering how he had gotten into the water in the first place. Was he diabetic? Septic? An accidental overdose of his medication, maybe?

With the tube around him, the three of us were ready to try and start swimming him to the beach. The woman was calm and managing to battle through the current and undertow and grabbed the pole extended to us from above by the doctor.

"Here you go guys, nice and easy," the doctor said.

We inched our way along. I was closest to the dock, and we struggled to keep the current from slamming me into the wooden pillars as we continued to reassure the confused man. Then the tube popped. The man became dead weight and his head slipped beneath the water. I kicked furiously to support the man's increasing weight. I noticed an increasing amount of blood in the water. Had he been stabbed? Shot? Is that how he ended up here? I did a quick trauma sweep of his chest and abdomen but did not feel or see any holes or entry wounds. The blood swirled around and eddied in the gaps of water between our bodies. As I readjusted my position to obtain a better hold of him, I realized I was the source of the blood. The slamming and banging against the dock had inflicted large lacerations on my arms, back, and feet.

We were only maybe forty feet from shore.

"Let's get going, let's just keep moving!" I attempted to remain calm, but I felt fear build inside of me. With my blood in the water and all the thrashing around, I thought about the danger of sharks.

As I was about to hit the end of my emotional and physical endurance, I felt my bloodied feet brush against the sandy bottom. A crowd of people rushed towards us to help drag the man to shore. They draped towels over the shivering man while the doctor performed a quick evaluation, others removing his wet clothes. He was somewhat delirious, but conscious, safe, and alive.

I examined my own wounds. Blood ran down my limbs. There

were multiple gashes across my back and on both feet. I was dabbing at the blood with towels, watching red stain the white fabric when my mom rushed up, panic-stricken.

She calmed quickly, despite the amount of blood pouring from various parts of my body.

"I'm very proud of you," she said, smiling and hugging me.

We spent the morning bandaging my wounds, which became more and more painful when the adrenaline wore off. They were jagged and gross-looking and stung under the warm water of the shower. At a small clinic on Sanibel Island, a doctor cleaned and bandaged my wounds and wrote me a prescription for antibiotics, a precaution for infections that might be caused by marine organisms. The doctor instructed us that both the pool and ocean were now off limits for me.

It was by this end that consequently, my marathon preparation also suffered as it became teeth-clenchingly painful to run with the deep cuts on my feet. The long, majestic oceanside runs that I had previously envisioned became excruciating trots. But my *because I said I would* promise pushed me through. By the time we returned to New England, there were five weeks until the Boston Marathon.

● ● ●

The weeks passed in an instant because of a mountain of schoolwork and an intensifying training regimen. The week before the race, news about the marathon was everywhere. "Boston Strong" was plastered on banners and signs all over the state as we prepared to "take back" Patriot's Day.

I was getting nervous again. I'd soon be back in Boston for a rerun of the worst day of my life. The anxiety for my family grew in parallel. They had all been on Boylston Street when the attack occurred, witnessing the explosions and the terror that followed. It wasn't until race weekend that my mom made the decision to join my dad at the finish line. However, I still struggled with the guilt of putting my loved ones in harm's way the previous year. The nightmares never stopped.

As I walked around campus in early April, I exchanged high fives with friends who knew I was running the marathon. It was a constant topic of conversation. The terrorists had failed, making the Boston Marathon larger and even more cherished than before. They had created an even stronger bond between runners, spectators, and the people of Boston.

Yet my brain often wandered to a dark place when I was alone in my dorm room, or by myself in the car. As the anxiety grew, there were regular late night phone calls to my mom and dad, during which I openly wondered whether I could actually summon the nerve to go to the city for the race on April 21st, my dad's birthday. With their support, and my *because I said I would* promise, I knew I would be there at the starting line.

I woke up on race morning feeling intensely nervous but also excited to run for the first time I could remember since the bombing. Exhilaration trumped my fear. As he had done the year before, my father drove me into Boston to catch the bus to Hopkinton. The city was quiet on our predawn drive in, but the people were present in those banners and "Boston Strong" signs that adorned the waking city. When my dad dropped me off downtown the energy was like nothing I had felt in my life.

When I arrived at the starting line, tears began to flow for the first of many times that sunny Monday. Spectators behind the barricades were four deep in some sections, yelling and screaming, thanking the runners, and holding up signs honoring the memories of Martin Richard, Krystle Campbell, Lu Lingze, and Sean Collier, the four who had been killed in the attack the year before.

I felt nerves creep back in as the crowd grew larger around me. So many people, so many bags, so much opportunity to inflict destruction. My eyes darted back and forth across the crowd and a cold sweat ran down my back.

"Stop it," I said to myself. This was not how I wanted to remember the day. I was running for so many people who believed in me. I had put everything into my training. I sure as hell was not going to let the terrorists ruin this day for me again.

That day I ran probably one of my worst marathon times ever, but I didn't care in the slightest. I spent half the race in tears. The crowds, the sights, the sounds, the feelings were burned into my heart and memory, where they would remain forever. The runners and spectators had united in a beautiful act of love and defiance. My hand was sore from high fives, my muscles ached from the distance, and I was overwhelmed by it all.

At the Boston College campus, students held out beers for the runners. As I did the year before, I grasped a can of Bud Light held out from a hand in the crowd and cracked the top, hearing the cheers of the crowd as I poured it down my throat. A police office in uniform cheered, clapped, and flashed me a thumbs-up. It occurred to me that this might be the only time in my life where a cop would applaud my underage drinking.

I finally arrived at the spot near the finish line where I had heard the first explosion the year before, the place where my life took such a dramatic turn. It was this spot, on this pavement, where my life had changed entirely. Choking back tears, a flutter of panic pulsed through my body causing my steps to falter. This exact area had been the start of each nightmare I had experienced since the bombing. Every detail was so ingrained into my deeper conscious that I could recall the cracks in the sidewalk, the bricks on the steps, the street signs, and flowers on the windowsills.

In a funny way though, being there gave me a new energy as my fight or flight response soared. The pain and horror of the previous year started to fade as it began to sink in that it was actually happening. I was going to finish the Boston Marathon this time. The noise from the crowd grew louder and louder as I turned onto Hereford Street. Next came a quick left turn onto Boylston and I caught my first glimpse of the finish line.

I removed my sunglasses to get the clearest possible view of what

I was about to experience. A sea of runners, most dressed in blue and yellow, surrounded me. We were all pushing to the end. Cheers from both sides of Boylston Street were deafening as fans held their signs high and the flags rippled in the breeze. For more than a year, this moment was my first thought upon awakening in the morning and the last thing on my mind before I fell asleep at night. Tears streamed down my face as I gathered speed. All physical pain and exhaustion had fallen away.

I saw dozens of police officers at the finish line and I'm sure that most runners and spectators were somewhat on edge, but then I heard someone yell my name, so I looked up into the stands and caught sight of my mom and dad. I'll never forget the smiles on their faces as they watched me fulfill my dream.

I raised my hands high above my head and took those final steps across the finish line. Someone placed the marathon medal around my neck and I rushed to find my parents. The three of us wept as we embraced, then left for a restaurant where we would be joined by other friends and relatives. My mom had baked a cake and we all raised our glasses.

I wish there was more of a Hollywood ending, but reality tends to intrude on even the most joyous experiences. A week after the marathon, I was again jolted awake in a cold sweat in my dorm room. It was another nightmare of the bombing, which I thought would stay safely in my past after finally achieving my goal. I had hoped to obtain closure. *Would it just take more time?* I was starting to wonder, even with the powerful memories of my second Boston Marathon experience.

I chose to try and focus on the positives, namely all the people who had supported me on this long journey—my family and friends. There was one name in particular that came to mind: Alex Sheen.

I found Alex's email address on the *because I said I would* website. It was honestly difficult to put my gratitude toward him into words. Had it not been for his inspiring TED Talk, I probably would not have been able to overcome my fears and run the Boston Marathon. As I wrote to Alex and revisited the strength of emotion of that day, tears once again rolled down my face. When I clicked send, I felt that my duty was done. I certainly never expected a reply from a person of Alex's stature. I resumed my studies for final exams and finally headed off to bed.

The next morning, I was shocked to see the name Alex Sheen in my inbox. In his short note, Alex said he wanted to set up a time to speak on the phone so he could hear my story. I was awestruck.

I was nervous when I dialed Alex's number at the appointed time the following week. My hands were shaky and sweating and I prayed my voice wouldn't tremble. Alex had become a hero to me and now he was interested in hearing my story.

Then he answered and sounded like just another human being.

"Hey Bobby," he said. "I just wanted to talk to you about your email. This is what *because I said I would* is all about. I'd really appreciate it if you could share your whole story with me from the beginning."

So I did. I told him about seeing the Boston Marathon jacket and the silliness of how it motivated me to attempt to run a marathon, and how I had earned a spot in the race through my fundraising efforts for Boston Children's Hospital. In as much brutal detail as my post-trauma mind could manage, I described the day of the marathon bombing and the repercussions on my family and me. I told him about the demons I had been facing and how his talk and the mission of *because I said I would* inspired me to complete the Boston Marathon and fulfill my promise no matter how difficult it had been.

I was out of breath and teary when I finished.

"Wow," Alex said.

He thanked me for using his cards and mission in the way I did. He expressed his concern for my family and admiration for our mental toughness. Then came something I wasn't expecting.

"This September in Columbus, Ohio we're having the first *because I said I would* conference. We're gathering people from around the country to share some of the most inspiring stories. This is the first time we've done this, and I would really like for you to be one of the main stage speakers if you're up for it?"

Without even thinking, I said yes. How could I not? My public speaking hero had just asked me to deliver a talk at his event so, shocked as I was, I accepted Alex's invitation in a heartbeat.

"Great," Alex said. "All you need to do really is tell your story, but we need a theme. Not everyone is a marathon runner, so how can we relate this to everyone? And what did you learn from this that you would want an audience to be inspired by? These are the things you need to think about. Keep it to around fifteen minutes. I'll work with you to develop the whole thing, nothing to stress about."

I thanked Alex for everything he had done for me and for the opportunity he had now put before me. I immediately called my parents and told them what had just happened. In four months, I'd be speaking at a huge conference in Ohio. They were thrilled. My dad enthusiastically told me to get cracking on the speech. That's how I spent my summer, writing and rewriting my speech, and then practicing it until it was seared into my brain.

The theme gave me trouble. The cliché anecdote about the marathon with the endurance message of, "life's not a sprint, it's a marathon" was cheesy and not necessarily relatable to many people. I was finding it hard to properly focus on reflecting back to the event and its aftermath, my brain doing anything it could to protect me from the distress this inflicted each time. I took a long walk in the White Mountains of New Hampshire to think about how the past two years had affected me. It was a painful exercise. I remembered my fear vividly. Terrorists had tried to paralyze the runners and spectators of the marathon with the use of fear, and they had very nearly succeeded with me. In so many ways I was still afraid, but I had run the marathon and finished despite my overwhelming apprehension.

That instantly became my theme, not letting fear keep you from living your life and stopping you from doing the things you love. It could be any kind of fear, large or small: giving blood despite a fear of needles; asking for a date despite a fear of rejection; and, fittingly, talking to a big crowd, despite a fear of public speaking.

Class presentations in high school and college were the extent of my experience speaking to groups. Even those talks were terrifying to me. Alex helped me prepare my speech to become concise and empowering, but never told me the size of my audience. It's probably better that I didn't know. As I began my junior year of college, practicing my talk was part of my daily routine. I was as ready as I would ever be by the time September came around.

I learned about some of the other speakers in YouTube promotion videos that *because I said I would* had posted about the conference. Many were well-known figures, like Alex, leading me to feel I had no business being on the same program. When my family and I finally flew to Ohio, I met the man behind it all in person.

Alex moved with a presence that commanded the attention of those around him. Tall in stature, his clean and trim appearance paired with a friendly smile made him easily likeable. The conversation that flowed confidently from his mouth had you hanging on to every word.

From that first meeting, I knew I wanted to be more like him.

I was stunned when the two of us walked through the doors of the Greater Columbus Convention Center, and my eyes widened in both amazement and fear. The space was massive. Tables were clothed in white. Blue and purple lights illuminated the walls and ceiling. The stage glowed in powerful spotlights. The words *"because I said I would"* were spread across clear glass behind the podium centered on the stage. The rows of chairs seemed to be endless.

I interrupted Alex while he was talking to another speaker, Garth Callaghan.

"How many, uh, people are going to be here tomorrow?" I asked.

"Hopefully just over a thousand," Alex replied, and then nonchalantly turned back to his conversation with Garth.

I was not doing this. No way in hell was I doing this. I smiled at Alex and tried to conceal my rising panic. Walking back to our hotel, I pictured myself in front of all those people, forgetting every word of the speech that I had so carefully prepared and practiced over the last four months.

"Dad, I can't do it," I said, throwing my arms up. "That is so many people."

My parents sat calmly on the bed.

"You do realize the irony here, don't you?" Dad asked.

"Tomorrow, you're going to give a speech about not letting fear control your life, and now you're afraid to do it." He smiled and laughed as he finished the sentence.

The next morning, I was too nauseous to eat. I had this terrible vision of needing to pee in the middle of my talk, but I was chugging water because my mouth was so dry. At the convention center, I found a program and looked at the list of speakers and topics. Garth was a published author who had made several appearances on national television. I saw the name of a new friend, Parker Schenecker, who had overcome terrible tragedy beyond words. I was scheduled to speak in the early afternoon, right after a person named Eva Kor.

Eva Kor was an eighty-year-old Holocaust survivor, whose twin was also at the Auschwitz concentration camp. At the age of ten, her twin sister Miriam and herself were transported from their village to Auschwitz. Her other two siblings and both of her parents were killed. Eva and her sister survived because they were experiment subjects of one of the most infamous and terrible Nazis, Dr. Josef Mengele. Eva had made a promise, when first imprisoned, that she would do everything in her power to keep her sister and herself alive. Eva looked after and cared for her sister until they were released in January 1945.

Decades later, Eva found it within herself to forgive her tormentor, a seemingly impossible and courageous act that was narrated in the 2006 documentary, *Forgiving Dr. Mengele*. And now a college kid with no speaking experience would have to follow her talk.

I sat in the audience and listened intently to Eva's gentle voice as she told her unimaginable tale. Somehow she managed to infuse humor into her talk, igniting laughter with her witty jokes. Other times she had most of her audience in tears. By the time she was finished, we were all emotionally spent.

Alex came on stage and thanked Eva for her incredible strength and courage, and the promise that she had made and kept to her sister. I began to sweat as the seconds ticked away until I would take my place on that same stage. Alex introduced me.

I felt every eye on me as I walked from my seat to the stage. At first I could feel my knees tremble under the weight of a colossal room full of stares. My throat became dry as I attempted to swallow, willing my body to make any progress towards the stage. Sweat trickled along the crease of my forehead and into the small of my back, dampening my white shirt. When my body finally carried itself forward, it was a surreal feeling; one of those moments where you can't really feel yourself walking but you're still moving forward. Almost like a dream, my actions felt involuntary. I fumbled to turn on the switch of my hands-free microphone, adrenaline robbing me of all dexterity.

Suddenly, without quite knowing how I got there, I was on stage, in a room filled with a thousand silent, expectant people. I had practiced the first lines of my talk hundreds of times so this moment would be almost an automatic response and I wouldn't freeze. It was time well spent. After those first few seconds, I felt my nerves gradually evaporate as things flowed in a way I had never imagined.

It's an amazing thing to stand in front of an audience, completely still and silent because of the story you are telling. A picture of the scene of the bombing flashed across the screen behind me. "This is fear," I said. "This is what thousands of people including my family witnessed on April 15, 2013." I fed off the energy of the faces staring up at me. My incredibly personal story was now being told to the thousand people in front of me, but I did not quiver as I narrated them through my pain. A photo of the memorial of shoes created in Boston days after the bombing appeared behind me, and I felt my voice rise, charged with the power of emotion. "Runners from around the world, including myself, laced their shoes around these rails and it was a message. It was a statement to the world that we will not be defeated, that we will not let those who hate and commit acts of evil in this world stop us from doing the things we love." I noticed people in the audience brushing away tears. "I did not let fear win. I did not let fear stop me from doing what I love, and I hope that you don't either." I spoke my last words, closed my eyes, and then reopened them to a thunderous standing ovation. I remember walking off the stage and shaking the hand of Alex as he moved toward the podium to announce an intermission.

My bladder was ready to explode and I rushed to the bathroom, but members of the audience began to stop me, some of them in tears, many of them saying my words had inspired them to stop letting fear run their lives: a person who had been afraid to run a 5K race with friends for fear of embarrassment was now going to do it; a person afraid to leave an abusive relationship would not let fear rule her decision-making; a young man told me that from this day forward he was going to stop using heroin. I was astounded. If only one person had benefitted from my story, that would have been enough, but seven people stopped to tell me their story on the way to that bathroom.

That day at the conference was, and still is, a very proud one for me, proof that as ordinary people our stories have the power to do good. Speaking that day had been my focus for months and, as with re-running the marathon, I had begun to see it as the one thing that would fix me. Yet as time passed, my own battles with fear and trauma remained far from over. Although speaking and physically acting out the intention I had brought to that speech, emotionally I was nowhere near the fearless and successful figure I had projected that day. I felt a longing for the person I had been before the bombing, and frequently angry at being robbed of this. I knew I needed to make some big changes in my life, to rediscover myself, and to run again for the sheer joy and pleasure of it.

It was time for me to start moving in a different direction, to act on my dreams, and search for freedom from the fear I felt was slowly destroying me.

CHAPTER THREE

RANCH OF HOPE

Jiquilillo, Nicaragua
January 2015

I had felt certain that finally finishing the Boston Marathon would vanquish my demons and put an end to the lingering trauma from the bombing. In that regard, I was bitterly disappointed. Nightmares of the bombing continued to intrude on my sleep. Running remained not a joy but a chore and a reminder of the worst day of my life. I was feeling more and more hopeless, trapped in that day. If finishing the marathon wasn't the cure, what would be? It began to seem like a radical change would be needed to stop the visceral and mental memories of that day from dominating my present life.

Fate seemed to provide an answer. To earn my paramedic degree, I was working at Speare Hospital in Plymouth, New Hampshire. There I learned about an upcoming medical mission trip to Nicaragua. By the time of the trip I would be a fully licensed paramedic. It immediately caught my eye and became the catalyst for a powerful stirring inside me. A yearning to see the world had simmered within me for some time, but I had never had the courage to make that first leap outside the boundaries of the United States. What if this was the radical change that I needed to reset my mind and my life? Maybe I could escape from the daily reminders and experience something completely foreign to me. Maybe I could combine my desire to travel with my hope to reclaim my passion for running.

With a little coaxing, I convinced my dad to join me. It would also be a completely new experience for him, a guy who had witnessed and contributed so much in forty years as an emergency room nurse. So on a cold January morning, my mom drove us to Logan Airport in Boston for my first trip out of the country.

I was surprisingly unafraid. My naivety about international travel saved me from much of the normal stress that would accompany such a trip. At the very least, I had done a bit of research and was prescribed anti-malaria pills. It was after dark when we arrived in the capital city of Managua and were ushered into a cramped shuttle, setting out for the Pacific Coast. In the headlights I could make out the outlines of palm trees, the first hint that we were now in the tropics, far away from the frigid mountains of New Hampshire. After three hours, the shuttle turned off the blacktop onto a bumpy dirt road.

In the headlights I could see a building with a straw roof, which I learned was part of a remote coastal hostel, Rancho Esperanza, in a village named Jiquilillo. I heard the waves crashing as we stepped from the van, and the faint sound of an acoustic guitar carried by the wind. Hammocks swayed in the breeze and I felt the thick warm air on my skin. We were greeted by Nate, a tall man with a long black ponytail who was the founder and owner of the hostel, but had grown up in a small town in Maine.

Nate explained he had come to Nicaragua in 2001 as part of a non-governmental agency to help alleviate endemic health and hygiene problems in the country. He returned two years later after Hurricane

Mitch destroyed many of the coastal towns and villages. Nate's group worked for months to rebuild what was left of a health clinic, but afterwards Nate saw there was so much work yet to be done. He stayed behind, finding his way to the tiny, impoverished fishing village of Jiquilillo.

By appearances alone, Jiquilillo is a slice of tropical seaside paradise, but the beautiful surface is tragically deceiving. Unfortunately it is plagued by alcoholism, domestic violence, and sexual abuse. Its people suffer from diabetes, malaria, hypertension, heart disease, poor diet, lack of education, and cheap alcohol perpetuating generations of suffering.

That is why Nate chose to stay. He bought a small plot of land and built the first cabana, then another and another, and soon had created Ranch Esperanza, "Ranch of Hope." He hired local people and began buying local food and produce to feed his guests. Nate and his girlfriend Shana had also created the Kid's Club, an after-school program for children in dangerous home environments. They organized art projects, soccer games, surfing lessons, and even taught children how to repair surfboards so they could earn money of their own. Word of the hostel spread among Central American backpackers and people from all around the world came to see it for themselves. The children met an eclectic mix of adventurers from all over the world, opening their eyes to opportunities never previously imagined.

Now our contingent was ready to chip in, bringing in medical supplies, which would include the first defibrillator in the village. We would also be teaching a course in first aid that Nate hoped to offer the entire village and the kids' club.

I was immediately curious to see what passed for healthcare in this tiny coastal village. The day after our arrival, a small Nicaraguan woman guided us down the road to a rusty structure that appeared relatively unstable. This was the clinic, where a doctor saw patients once a week. It was a bumpy hour-long drive to the nearest hospital, and ambulances wouldn't respond to the village unless the person in need could pay for the fuel. In any event, it was a long hike to find a place with cell reception.

Nate served as the ambulance, driving those with medical emergencies to the hospital in his rusty pickup. The remote location and poor resources meant a heart attack could easily prove fatal.

The head of the "clinic" was a self-proclaimed healing woman with no formal medical training. She and her assistants functioned on a patchwork blanket of knowledge and skills learned from others over the years, leading to a moderately dysfunctional system. However, these passionate individuals cared deeply for their community and made what they had work for them as best they could. I inspected their supplies and spoke to them in broken Spanish, trying to not cringe. The place was covered in a film of dust, and most supplies and medications were disintegrating within their packages.

For someone who had never traveled outside the United States before and had the benefit of growing up in a suburban middle-class family, it was an eye-opening experience to say the least.

In my short time in Jiquilillo, I found myself spending less and less time with my traveling companions. This was mainly the fault of my fascination with the other travelers that I was meeting at the communal dinners each night. For the first time in my life I was conversing with people from around the world. I was energized by their experiences and stories, lives that were so different than my own. They seemed to have lived a thousand lives in the space of my one. I wanted to be like them.

At Rancho, dinner each night was served at long and sturdy wooden tables. These had been built by German carpenters a few years back as payment for a place to stay on their travels. That sort of barter was not uncommon. A group of Dutch artists, as another example, had painted beautiful murals on the walls of the cabañas to pay their board.

I loved everything about Rancho Esperanza, and felt old inhibitions falling away in a surprisingly easy fashion. This even stretched to my palate. I hated seafood growing up, but now found myself enjoying some of the freshest fish you could ever imagine.

One night at dinner, over a bottle of rum, I met a Norwegian girl named Hanne, who was backpacking with a friend through Central America. Hanne and I stayed up talking long after the others had drifted off to bed. We took the rum to the pristine and empty beach and sparked up a fire. We spent the night there, talking, drinking, laughing, and staring at the brightest stars I had ever seen, no light pollution to limit their radiance.

At times we listened silently to waves crashing onto the beach. I remember the wet sand between my toes, the smoky smell in the air, and the bright reflection of fire against Hanne's tanned face.

English was one of the four languages that Hanne spoke fluently. We talked about everything. I had never felt that deep a connection with another person before, and much less with someone I had known for only a few hours. Perhaps this was the reward of travelers, an interconnectedness that blesses people with free spirits. This was just my first taste of it.

A pink sun began to peek over the horizon. The fishing boats returned from the sea as the dawn broke and we reluctantly decided to get a few hours of sleep. My group would be leaving Jiquilillo in a few hours, but I desperately wanted to stay. In my few nights here, there were no nightmares, and no thoughts of the bombing intruded on my waking hours. For the first time since April 2013, I felt that my mind, body, and soul were healing. Was this just a break from the reality to which I would soon return, or could experiencing these new landscapes, challenges, and people be the key to finding peace?

I kissed Hanne on the cheek as I boarded our bus, saying goodbye with the conviction that I would see both her and Rancho Esperanza again.

Our bus wound back over the twisting dirt roads, through small jungle villages, to the loud and polluted city of Chinandega. Our mission in this city—located in the center of the country and with a population of 200,000 people—was to deliver training to fire and ambulance crews.

We were very warmly greeted by our Central American colleagues inside the station. Upon investigation they had plenty of equipment, but limited knowledge of how to use it. This was a valuable lesson on sustainable aid. Developed countries generously donate medical supplies and equipment, but with little training on their use, the benefit to these countries and their services can be lost.

After a few days in Chinendega, our group planned on spending some days relaxing in Grenada. I saw this as a chance to strike out on my own. I spoke with my dad, who had also fallen in love with Jiquilillo, and convinced him that I spoke enough Spanish to get us back there without getting lost or killed. We informed the others of our plan to return to Rancho Esperanza the next morning. It would be my first experience of spontaneity while traveling and it deepened my thirst for adventure.

Sharing this moment with my father is something I will always cherish and it fortified an already strong bond between us. We were seeing, experiencing, and feeling new things, and he was witnessing a change within me that would be difficult to explain to anyone else.

When we branched away from our travel companions I was still incredibly nervous. After two transfers on a "chicken bus," and a ride in an unlicensed taxi, we made it back to Jiquilillo by dinnertime the next day. I vowed to make the most of every second at the place I had grown to love in such a short period of time. A completely different group of travellers were now staying at the hostel and I recognized how much people mean to a place in these situations. While traveling you can never recreate an experience, you just have to enjoy the present moment for what it is. As was true the first time, the people I met on my second visit were amazing. Robbie and Mickey were a couple in their late twenties from Chicago. Both had thriving professional careers but became unhappy and bored with a traditional lifestyle. So they quit their jobs, sold much of their belongings, left their apartment, and began a two-year adventure around the world. At the time I did not realize what a profound influence they would end up having on my own choices; showing me the possibilities of stepping outside a conventional life.

My love for Rancho and Jiquilillo only deepened as the days

went on. I pray a hotel chain or real estate developer never discovers Jiquilillo. Unfortunately, it is a sad pattern repeated in developing countries all over the world. Luxury hotels are constructed in these beautiful, serene places for the rich and affluent to explore exotic locales. What happens then is tragic. Unspoiled beauty is lost, along with local customs and cultures. I am fully aware it is a catch-22. These resorts often bring jobs to the community, potentially raising the standard of living. Local people experience the wealth and glamour of American life, and it's natural that they would try to find it for themselves. And why? Because they want to feel important and respected. Exposure to a more consumerist culture and lifestyle will ultimately make those who do not partake feel lesser, or judged, for not having those things so highly prized in this other way of life.

This taught me another lesson in my travels; an important one that I always try to keep close to heart. We need to do a better job at making people feel important and respected for who they are, not who they think they should aspire to be.

There's a bit of irony here though, and this is where I'm going to make a small argument that may initially sound marginally counterintuitive and that plays on generalizations that of course will not apply to every individual. My belief is that people in developing countries are sometimes happier with what little they have, than us Americans with everything we do have. Over time, in developed countries, materialism became a priority. Having things meant having money, having money meant power, power meant status, and status correlated to happiness. There was a shift from focusing on all that we do have, to everything we don't. When people thought about what they didn't have, they connected that to their self-worth. Many people relate low mood or dissatisfaction with life to not having the best car or house, the newest things, or the most money. As humans in the developed world, we live in a very comparative and competitive society. This can drive us to achieve our best, but can also bring out the worst. I attribute a lot of this now to social media. We judge ourselves based on how others look, what others have, or what they do, and use these observations to place a value on ourselves.

People in Nicaragua do not live in as comparative a society as is commonplace in developed countries. They are more appreciative for what they have than they are troubled by what they do not. Desire for money and wealth is outweighed by an appreciation for those things that allow them to simply live each day.

It was while reflecting on these new views of the world that it clicked for me how rare and authentic an experience I was having. Just from completely opening my eyes, ears, and heart to something entirely foreign to me, I was learning things that would have remained hidden from me if I relied on the pages of a book or the depths of the internet. Traveling is what I wanted, by teaching me to act and behave in ways that I never had before it was beginning to help me heal. This feeling electrified and excited me, I finally felt that I was making progress in becoming myself again; or more truthfully, I was transforming into a new person but one that I was happier with. I had to let go of the desire for everything to "go back to normal" when I realized there was no way of returning to the person I was before the bombing. Now I was discovering that perhaps that could be a positive. By the end of my trip, I was not putting on a fake smile and saying that everything was fine; this time it was truly genuine.

Each day, I ran on the beach at sunrise as the waves gently lapped against the sand. Here I could once again appreciate the motion as something primitive, pure, and beautiful. Just running. No more, no less. I felt my love for it beginning to creep back; a small glimmer that burned slowly brighter with every mile.

I never wanted that first trip to end. I knew I needed to travel, to revel in the physical beauty of foreign places, and in the wisdom of people from around the world. I needed to run in these remote jungles, high mountains, and untouched beaches; to run wild in the most basic and primitive sense. I had hope. I knew what needed to be done. When I returned to snowy New Hampshire in the dead of winter, I booked another plane ticket.

CHAPTER FOUR

BLUE MOUNTAINS

Katoomba, New South Wales, Australia
May 2015

My iPhone rang out in a chorus of bothersome alarms, but the rhythmic swaying of the boat impeded my ability to open my eyes. Groggily, my hand found the phone stuffed deep under my pillow and silenced the device beckoning me to begin the day. It took several slow seconds for me to regain my bearings. Looking up, the ceiling appeared closer to my face than normal causing a brief spell of confusion only exacerbated by the lingering jet lag.

My brain was slow to boot up that morning, but finally was able to connect the dots. It wasn't a ceiling intruding on my personal space; it was the old wooden planks of the bunk above me. This was my second morning in Australia but my first aboard a boat, sixty kilometers off the coast, in the South Pacific. Diving the Great Barrier Reef was on that same bucket list from eighth grade which saw me dreaming of running the Boston Marathon, and it was now my turn to live out the former. It had been four months since my epiphany in Nicaragua, and I had wasted no time acting upon it, now finding myself about as far away from home as I could possibly be.

My legs wobbled as I swung them over the edge of the bed and onto the freshly carpeted floor. My toes gripped at the cushiony surface and I stood up, bracing myself in case the ship should suddenly lurch. Steady enough, I made my way out the door and up into the galley for a morning snack before the first dive.

I blinked against the brilliant sunlight on the deck and groggily waved hello to some of the exuberant Europeans down the hall that were already set to jump in the water. Scuba diving, similar to running and endurance sports, attracts some of the most passionate people you will ever meet. Both of these sports share an inexplicable motivating factor, the mystique of exploration leading to a perpetual thirst for more.

A quick slice of toast (no vegemite) and a fresh banana with a bowl of cereal was the perfect amount of nourishment for my morning dive. My bunkmate and dive buddy, Vincent, entered the room and took a seat next to me. Vincent was an enthusiastic German not much older than me. His friendly and outgoing personality made us fast friends early into our trip out to the reef. After months of travel around the world, he had made his way down to Australia following an incredible trek through Southeast Asia that made my mind race with future travel plans. Stories of the jungles of Cambodia, Laos, and Vietnam stoked my lust for adventure in a land becoming increasingly popular with backpackers.

For now, I was more than content with the adventure at hand, exploring the world's largest coral reef, one that stretched for over 2,300 kilometers, made up of more than 2,900 individual reefs; a scuba diver's dream.

Today was finally the day to plunge below the surface into a magical ecosystem unlike any other in the world. Vincent and I moved out to the stern of the boat where all the scuba equipment was meticulously organized and stored. We began to suit up, first putting on the protective "stinger suit" that covers any exposed skin to deter a painful encounter with the ample amount of jellyfish that call the GBR home.

My hands were almost shaking with excitement as I pulled my buoyancy control device tight over my shoulders, tightening one strap and then another.

Vincent was almost finished strapping his fins on when he looked up at me with a huge smile on his face. "Are you ready for this?" The way his voice pitched at the end revealed the unmistakable excitement that matched my own.

"I've been waiting a long, long time for this. C'mon, let's get in the water!" I made my way down to the lower platform to perform my buddy check.

On the boat's lower platform, I squinted against the glint of the morning sun on the water. There was no land in any direction, and it was absolutely beautiful. I thought about the night before, when a few of us had sat on the roof deck of the vessel and marveled at the stunning brightness of the stars, the Southern Cross spread out like a beacon across the black canvas. That moment was perfectly peaceful, so far away from home, in the middle of the ocean with no sound but the calm slaps of the waves rhythmically tapping the hull. The cool evening breeze was just the right temperature to be comfortable in a hoodie, and was a welcome reprieve from the daytime humidity. It was perfect.

I had never been so far from home, but had never felt safer and more in tune with my surroundings. Taking a leap of faith straight out of my comfort zone was allowing me to experience the immense beauty of the world, the bonus was that I also seemed to be letting go of some of the horror that had settled into my daily life. There were no thoughts of bombings, or terror, or hate. Instead, my mind and heart were filled with awe for the beauty of our delicate planet. That deep peace was an affirmation for me, a nod that I had been right to seek out a different path and to pursue a life of adventure in such distant places, a life unthinkable to me only a few years before. As a result, days would pass between thoughts of the bombing. Crowds and cities no longer terrified me. It seemed as if beauty and adventure were expelling the pain from my tattered heart. I was wholly in my element, waking up in the morning eager for what each day would bring.

"You ready man? Don't keep me waiting now!" Vincent's voice snapped me out of my reverie. He had his hand on my shoulder, mask on his face and ready to jump.

He smirked and took a leap off the platform into the welcoming turquoise water.

Before his head could break the surface, I followed suit and was immediately caressed by the gentle and soothing touch of the ocean. A quick "okay" signal later and the two of us descended down to seven meters to equalize our ears and make sure everything was functional before leaving the shadow of the boat.

The ritualistic briefing before the dive had been light-hearted and comical with a cheery South African providing basic information on Flynn Reef. His schematic diagram on the whiteboard was plentiful with cartoonish clownfish and turtles as well as useful distances, routes, and depths. Vincent and I had made a game plan based off this quick meeting, deciding to do a simple out and back for our first dive of the eleven we would have whilst on the boat.

A few short kicks and we were off on a bearing of thirty degrees to one of the larger reef arrangements. The water visibility was spectacular, like nothing I had ever dove in before. It was no more than five minutes into our journey when the circular shape of a green sea turtle appeared from the perpetual blue beyond. Within another minute, a beautiful hawksbill turtle glided just past us toward the reef, almost crashing into us head-on. We followed him towards the coral formations where he had perched himself into a little nook, munching on the leafy vegetation for his morning breakfast.

Even through his mask, I could see the excitement in Vincent's eyes when he looked up at me. We were both super stoked. Even though turtles are very common on tropical dives, it wasn't any turtle—it was a Great Barrier Reef sea turtle. We were living a scene from *Finding Nemo*. We hovered close to him for a while, in truth much longer than we should have, causing us to reevaluate our original dive plan.

Bright beautiful corals, incredible rock formations, wonderfully colored fish, and a blue-spotted ray filled the rest of our almost hour-long dive. When we broke the surface back at the boat, our faces were a perfect reflection of our experience.

"I'd say it went well!" the dive master yelled from the platform looking down at the stupid grins on both our faces.

Clambering up the ladder, we began to strip our equipment off and checked back in with the cheery young deckhand who had logged everyone off the boat. It's probably a huge liability or something if you leave a person behind in the middle of the ocean.

The days diving on that boat were jam-packed, any fatigue quickly overcome by the absolute thrill every time we entered the water. Each site we went to was just as spectacular as the one before, if not better. From the smallest clownfish to the sleek and agile reef sharks, it was a true diver's paradise that felt like heaven to me.

We would dive three times a day including a night dive after dinner. The cooks would toss all the organic scraps off the stern, resulting in a feeding frenzy of fish, all under the display of the massive rear spotlight. Within minutes, fish would be pushed out of the way by some larger reef sharks that had just been hankering for some apples and curry.

Night dives were shorter, almost thankfully so, as by the end of the day exhaustion plagued our muscles and a cramped lower bunk very quickly became the next exciting adventure. Instead of escaping off to bed after one of the night dives, Vincent and I stayed up for a beer in the kitchen with a few of the others.

The conversation revolved mostly around diving and our backgrounds, but eventually changed into the nature of our travels. This is when Vincent said something profound enough that I will never forget it, partly because it sounds so counterintuitive until you really think about it.

When discussing being away for so long he said, "You know, the further I get from home, the more comfortable it is. I never really travel with friends, because I like the experience of meeting new people better, which can be tough to do when you are with someone familiar. When you know someone, it can create a comfort zone that you cling to. And it's not that I am a loner, it actually makes me reach out to befriend people even more. It's hard to be alone, when you travel alone."

It was that last line that got me. *It's hard to be alone, when you travel alone.* The statement sounds so backwards, but is one of the truest I have ever heard.

We are naturally social creatures that need and desire interaction with each other. When we are forced outside our comfort zone into a new environment or situation, we will seek out companionship to fulfill that comfort. That is why Vincent's remarks are spot-on. When traveling alone, I have met people that after knowing them for twenty-four hours, can be considered as some of my best friends. The connection between people who share these experiences runs deep and the bonds forged tend to endure. The people I've met are undoubtedly the greatest reward of my global adventures.

A few days later, I made my way to Sydney on a rather forgettable flight. Rain crashed onto the pavement as I read the public transit board outside of the airport. Thankfully, my hostel was close to one of the larger train stations downtown, making for a rather easy journey. Sydney also has some of the best public transport I have ever used in the world. Clean, fast, efficient, and on time; everything you wouldn't expect from a public system.

After checking in, I knew I needed to attempt a run, my legs itching to stretch out after days of being held captive at sea. The big draw of heading to Australia was a marathon I had signed up for which was now only three days away. That guilty feeling runners have when taking more than a couple of days off created a huge pit in my stomach. City running wasn't my favorite, but I figured I could suck it up and run down to the Circular Quay to see the Sydney Opera House and Harbor Bridge. Lacing my shoes up, I thought about the marathon ahead.

My first international race, and it was on the other side of the world in a secluded national park. It was also going to be my first ultra marathon and first experience of a largely unsupported race that required you to run with a pack and carry many of your own provisions. Needless to say, I was slightly overwhelmed. Each new detail of the event made it somewhat more intimidating to me. The North Face fifty kilometers is a trail race now known as Ultra-Trail Australia (UTA). Because I was traveling through Australia on my summer break from college, this was the only marathon in the country during my visit. When signing up I told myself, "Just five more miles than a marathon," closed my eyes, and hit the button to register.

The race was held in Katoomba, in the Blue Mountains National Park. UTA's website describes the race as, "Australia's most challenging, stunning, and prestigious trail running event."

I thought about the difficulty and unparalleled beauty that lay ahead of me this weekend while walking outside onto a soggy Sydney street. Kicking my feet back, I started my run and made it a whole fifty meters before getting stuck behind a whole slew of people at a crosswalk. *No worries, I'll wait it out,* my upbeat brain told my legs. The signal changed and I picked up the pace again, ducking and weaving through men and women dressed in raincoats and donning umbrellas. *Beep!* Cars honked and puddles splashed, composing an urban orchestra to add to my running playlist. *Bang,* the loud noise violently interrupted my careless thoughts, causing my stomach to turn on itself. A sweat, unrelated to the exertion of running, overtook my body and my heart rate spiked. Turning my head on a swivel, I registered the nonchalance of those around me, unaffected by the panic that had stricken my body. Then, off to the right down an alleyway, I spied a construction crew moving manhole covers, their metallic impact causing the brassy, clattering noises. It wasn't a bomb.

Even though I felt like I was making progress, the residual effects of the Boston Marathon bombing still cast a long shadow. This deeply seeded memory of fear still had the ability to immediately grip my mind and body in fight or flight mode, the shock felt fresh each time. The hold it still exerted over me played largely on my mind. Living in and going to college in a rather rural setting, I still had not had much city exposure aside from the occasional drive home from school where I would pass through Boston. No matter how much I wanted to be "normal" again, I had to be content with the fact that I was making progress.

Shaken but not deterred, I strode on another fifty meters before I stopped at yet another crosswalk and waited. This pattern repeated four more times before I gave up on the run for good. Although Sydney was great, it reaffirmed my bias against city running and made me look forward to the pastoral trails that I knew were in my future.

Fifteen minutes of walking at a brisk pace brought me to my first view of the Sydney Opera House. As someone with very minor interest in architecture, I was still tremendously impressed by what is one of the most iconic buildings in the world. As I approached the Opera House, the amazing detail of the paneling on the white shells became even more prominent. It is just as much a work of art as it is a functional building. I marveled at its perfect curves and abrupt points, looking up as I walked, embracing the iconic role of an American tourist. Soon rain began to thunder down from the dark clouds overhead, cutting my visit short and sending me scuttling to find a dry place to eat before the monotonous run back.

Once I returned to the hostel, I stripped down from my wet clothes and took my first legitimate shower in five days. Simultaneously, I performed the mental checklist in my head of what needed to be done before getting on the train bound for Katoomba tomorrow. *Brenda*, I thought. I totally forgot to email Brenda.

About a month before I departed for Australia, I received an email out of the blue from a woman named Brenda Cunningham-Lewis. She introduced herself to me as a local reporter for a small newspaper called the *Blue Mountains Gazette*. She noticed I was one of only a handful of Americans in the race and was curious about my reason for coming all the way to Australia for it. When I told her, she thought she struck journalism gold. Brenda then wanted to interview me regarding my experience at the Boston Marathon and what I was hoping to gain by running the race down through the Australian bush. We exchanged dozens of emails back and forth and eventually she even invited me to come for a home-cooked meal with her family after the race.

She was kind and compassionate, understanding that it was difficult for me to discuss the day of the bombing. As I had continually expressed that I was now traveling to escape and heal from the horrors of that day, I think she began to feel guilty about questioning me. On several occasions she cordially offered to cancel her story so I could simply enjoy my travel in Australia without stirring up bad memories. There was a comfort in talking to her about it though, someone who was so far removed from the event that I felt no sort of judgment or precedent of what was expected to be said. She was genuinely curious and sympathetic.

After my shower, I emailed her and told her about my estimated time of arrival in Katoomba. I realized that I was excited to see her. Then it was time to rest. On a Friday night in Sydney, I was asleep by nine o'clock.

My alarm woke me up early the next morning. Dazedly, my eyes caught up with my brain willing me to swing my legs over the top bunk. The slight shimmer of sunlight that peered in from the window revealed the chaos that was my room, and I was shocked I had slept through the night. Beer bottles, a half empty handle of vodka, a handful of nips, a one-hitter, and an array of clothes were scattered across the floor. Truth be told, if I weren't prepping for a grueling trail ultra marathon and catching an early train, I would have found myself right in the middle of it.

Slowly, I descended the ladder of the bunk, careful not to wake the girl tangled in a mess of sheets below me. One of my keys for an early travel day is to have everything packed the night before except my clothes for the day. That way, I wasn't creating heaps of noise rummaging through my bags, waking up exhausted and sometimes easily agitated hostel mates.

Within four minutes I was out the door and on my way to the train. My overpriced Australian coffee tasted exceptionally average as I made my way through the city, joining the daily migration of business-men and women. I can't say enough about how well the public transit is organized in New South Wales. Without much fuss I found my way to the proper train traveling outbound to Katoomba and tried to relax for the two-hour ride.

Trains scared me still. Not ever planes, or really buses, but trains seemed to have the ability to trigger panic in me. I remember vividly on the day of the marathon bombing how all public transport in Boston was immediately shut down, even the ever-running T. Many of the terror attacks across the world have also involved devastating train bombings. Every unattended bag scared me far beyond what would be considered rational, every fellow passenger morphing into a potential threat.

I hated that my brain worked like this now. It's never a bad thing to be self-aware, but being constantly suspicious is not healthy. The persistent reminder of how the Boston Marathon bombing affected my everyday life was cumbersome and unwelcome. Stubbornly, I continued with my mission to live a life unlimited by the terrorists who tried so hard to take away that freedom. I would not let them win, and I would not let fear control me.

Luckily, a good book and terrific scenery as the train rushed deeper into the heart of Australia made the ride fly by. Upon arriving at the much more rural train station, I felt nothing but excitement for the days ahead. A light breeze kissed my cheeks, welcoming me to the quaint town of Katoomba. According to the map, a brief bus ride to the other end of town would leave me just a short walk from my hostel.

That is, if I had taken the right bus. After seeking out some Wi-Fi to check Google Maps, I realized my error. I was not about to cough up the money for another bus fare, which would have equated to a small snack and a coffee later in the trip; my legs needed a stretch anyway. I approached a small gift store and asked the longhaired, tanned-skin man behind the counter for directions.

"Can I help ya?"

"Yeah, could you just point me the right way to get to the CMS Conference Center? The one next to that Scenic World area I think."

"Ah, of course, mate. Ya got a bit of a trek ahead of ya. See the cable tram?" He pointed out the window to a large yellow trolley moving slowly across a wire suspended high over the valley. "You want to go straight towards where that's heading. Follow the trailhead behind that building there and you should be seeing some signs for Scenic World. Can't be more than five to six kilometers."

"Cool man, thanks so much!"

"Cheers mate, good luck if you're running, it's a killer out there!"

When I left the store, I found a viewing deck that looked out over the valley I needed to cross to reach my bed for the night. The expansive beauty of the Blue Mountains National Park lay out before me like an image from a postcard. The entirety of the fifty-kilometer racecourse could be seen, and it did not look forgiving in the least. However, I was also willing to wager this would be the most magnificent place I had the pleasure of running so far.

What's more, I felt safe; the feeling of comfort was almost immediate once I left the city and got onto the trails, far removed from the urban jungle and masses of people. Less worry clouding my mind made the task of focusing on running infinitely easier, and I finally felt ready to enjoy a good run.

The hike through the valley was just as gorgeous as the view of it from above. Winding paths and gushing waterfalls, hidden behind dense brush, lent a magical feel to every forward step. After encountering a few other tourists out hiking and some other runners scouting the racecourse, I finally made it up above the tree line to a scattered mix of buildings and a paved road.

I immediately knew I was in the right place as extraordinarily fit-looking men and women passed by in all directions, lycra leggings and brightly colored trail shoes adorning their feet.

My hostel was a small church conference center directly across from the start and finish line, a perfect set-up for the early morning start to the race. Of my three bunkmates, two were Kiwis and one an Aussie, all with a significantly larger amount of trail and ultra experience than me. Chatting with them and absorbing all their advice for me began to soothe my nerves, despite the extraordinarily challenging race ahead. The Australian, Ian, was running the fifty-kilometer race while the Kiwis were attempting the one hundred-kilometer event.

One of them was a nice older gentleman named Kevin who was from Christchurch, a moderately sized city on the South Island, and he was eager to take me under his wing. He told me all about the errors first-time ultra runners make, and things to avoid and be wary of while running out in the Australian bush. He explained to me the benefit of walking up hills to conserve energy and how trail ultras like this one are the definition of the age-old adage of being a "marathon and not a sprint." This was all about being smart and monitoring your energy level. The more we talked, the more I got to know him and his background. His passion for running was striking, easily portrayed by the way he described his past races; the pure thrill of being outdoors and letting your body work to its full potential. It was really quite beautiful, another reminder of the real reasons running was so important to me. That conversation with Kevin felt significant to me; playing an important part in revealing some of the progress I was making.

He was originally from Ireland and spoke often about going back to visit friends and family. Although he had lived in New Zealand for a very long time, there was always a special place in his heart for his home country. The quality that truly impressed me about Kevin was his unreserved kindness towards everyone, and everything. As a twenty-one year old, by myself, on the other side of the world, and about to run the most difficult race of my life, Kevin could not have made me feel more calm and comfortable. This was especially obvious when explaining to me a crucial error that I naively overlooked when planning for this race.

We were commenting on the elevation profile and how I wasn't concerned as much about the climbs as I was the technical running skill required for some of the terrain.

"Have you done a lot of hill training, mate?"

"Not a ton, but sometimes I go a bit back home. I know that it's difficult, but it could be worse than 2,400 feet, right?"

There it was. My first ignorant American comment, and something I had been completely oblivious to when I first signed up for the race.

"Feet? That's not feet, Bobby. That's 2,400 *meters* of elevation gain." Kevin chuckled and grinned as he said this.

"Oh." I paused. "Well, I mean that's only a little more than triple what I thought it would be!" We both let out a big laugh.

The four of us wandered over to the opening ceremony where an aboriginal group were performing a tribal song and dance. The rhythm and beat was unlike anything I had heard before. A didgeridoo echoed and hummed perfectly with the pounding of animal hide drums. It was like an ancient pump-up song, prepping us for the big day just ahead.

I slept like a rock that night, contrary to what I had feared. I had envisioned a night of tossing and turning with the anticipation; not only of running my first race longer than a marathon, but now with the sudden surprise of increased elevation gain. Nonetheless, I slept soundly and peacefully, giving my muscles a final reprieve before the storm to come.

Cold was the first thing I felt when I woke up a few hours before the start of the race. Ian and I promised the other two Kiwis we would see them off at the earlier start of the one hundred-kilometer race. The energy was electric and so was the interaction between all the competitors. Trail running was almost a totally different sport than its road-based counterpart. It felt more personal and connected, and there was more closeness between the athletes. I loved it, embracing this new domain unreservedly. This was exactly what I wanted if I was going to begin racing again, the kind of environment where I could thrive, and let my spirit recover.

When the time came for our race to begin it mirrored exactly what I had seen amongst the runners who had started a few hours before. It was absolutely amazing to be a part of. The horn buzzed loud and was echoed on by the whooping and shrieks of all the runners pumping their fists emphatically into the air. We were off.

The first few miles along the dirt roadways were an absolute breeze, but that all changed when we dropped down into the valley. The thick trees began to obstruct the sunlight as I cautiously ran down slippery rock and root, hopping down the bigger gaps. Rushing water could be heard around the bend and a massive waterfall appeared into view. The rivers that ran off of it lubricated the rocks; a recipe for disaster for the unassuming runner. On the valley floor, I ran as fast as the overhanging vines would allow. Although my mile pace was slower than normal, the proximity to the canopy of trees made it feel like my feet were flying over the rough terrain.

The trail was like a tunnel, enclosed by tall trees and plants, some that I had never seen before. It felt like a scene from *Jurassic Park*, sprinting through the woods with trees and vines in a blur all around me. It was a rush that made my heart beat faster than the natural increase from the surging adrenaline in my body. This was much different than the normal city concrete; this was exhilarating.

We would climb and then drop, climb and then drop, an endless game of counting the short intervals of flat ground that were few and far between. One climb brought us out onto a cliff edge that showcased a view of one of the park's crowning natural wonders, the Three Sisters. Three massive stone towers jutted out of the landscape, freestanding as if they were magical islands floating high above the valley.

I stared out at them in slack-jawed amazement until, *crash.*

Next I knew, I was on the ground on my hands and knees, the unmistakable feeling of a warm stream of blood running down my face. I was seeing stars and my vision blurred as pain seared through my head. In my ignorance, I had allowed my view to stray from the path for too long. My legs quickly ran out of instructions to follow from my brain's instinctive route planning. Ultimately this had led to me tripping on a rock, unfortunately managing to smash my face into a boulder on my way to meet the ground.

"You good, mate?" Almost instantly another runner was upon me, dropping to his knees with his hand upon my back.

"Yeah, yeah. Just a little startled." I tried to laugh but I was honestly just too embarrassed to say anything else.

"Well, make sure you get someone to check on that for you, ey?" He patted me on the back and continued on, leaving me to lick my wounds and swallow my pride.

I wiped my hand across my face, smearing the still-oozing blood from the gash across my forehead. In my mind it was presumably one of those injuries that just looked and felt worse than it actually was. So I pushed on.

Later, I found out I was much more fortunate than some of the other runners that day. That included one man who fell down a cliff and shattered his femur, warranting a more intensive and complex rescue. Thankfully the rest of my race wasn't nearly as eventful, my lesson quickly learned to be more attentive to my footing during a trail race.

While the miles went by, I found the race astoundingly peaceful, even therapeutic. I was not thinking of the city streets of Boston, or concerned about bombs, or terrorism. I loved running in these mountains and in this jungle. Nature flourished around me in a space that had a very primitive and ancient feel. Running here felt like something I was born to do. It was just me, my thoughts, and the trail. This sentiment felt like a huge step for me, one that brought me closer to finding peace with the events of April 2013. I felt a shift in my perspective, perhaps finally allowing me to once again appreciate the true, bare roots of the sport I had once loved. The first six and a half hours went by almost too fast for me, and before long I realized I had only one kilometer to go. Unfortunately I knew what that kilometer entailed.

A massive ascent up 951 stairs known as the Furber Steps was the last obstacle that stood between the finish line and me. One painful step at a time, I began my ascent. If you were to talk to anyone who has run this event now known as Ultra-Trail Australia, the one painful memory they will always regale you with is their experience on the Furber Steps. Of the many serendipitous moments I would experience on my travels, one was to eventually meet and become friends with the Scottish stone-mason responsible for building these steps years previously.

I crested the peak after an agonizing battle that made me never want to see a staircase again, and saw flat ground for the first time in ages. The blare of a loud speaker was so near that it pumped a newfound energy into my weary legs. This was my time to kick.

Moving as fast as my legs would carry me, I rushed towards the finish line and threw my hands high over my head, completing my first international ultra marathon in a time of just over seven hours. Almost immediately, I was whisked off by a group of people and was having my photo taken. My elated and endorphin-flooded brain was surprised to learn that they were with a few Australian media outlets, and for a few minutes I felt the closest I ever have to being a professional athlete.

What I did not know, was that I was one of the only Americans in the race and that the sentencing for the Boston Marathon bombers was this very day. Brenda's story about me in the *Blue Mountains Gazette* garnered increasing interest from other sources, wanting my take on the current situation. Brenda's husband was also there to greet me at the finish and handed me a cell phone number after introducing himself and showing me around the media area.

"Here you go mate. Talk to this bloke, he wants to do a story. The *Sydney Morning Herald*! That's like your *New York Times*! I've got to do some more coverage on the race, but let me introduce you to a few people first." He wrapped his arm around me and grabbed me a fresh bottle of water; the cool touch of the drink felt blissful against my salt-covered hands.

We walked into an office where he presented me to many of the race executives who all shook my hand and congratulated me. "Pretty tough for an American," one of them said as he winked at me. The whole finish experience was a whirlwind quite unlike anything I had expected.

"I best get back to work," he said to me as he removed a camera from the satchel bag at his side, "but I'll see ya at dinner later, okay Bobby?" He gave me the thumbs-up and I waved him off.

Exhausted but content, I made my way over to a green grassy hill, sat down, and pulled out my very simple and retro-looking Australian cell phone. My fingers shook as I dialed the number that he had jotted down for me. After a few rings, a reporter picked up the phone.

"Um, hi. This is Bobby O'Donnell. Someone gave me this number and said you wanted to talk to me?" I must've sounded like an idiot in my post-race delirium.

A thick Australian accent greeted me on the other end in an excited tone. "Yeah mate, great to hear from ya. Good run today?"

I sighed. "Yeah man, you got some hills out here, I'll tell you that much!"

He chuckled back. "Yep! But sure is beautiful in the mountains. Hey, now I won't keep ya too long. Just given your closeness to the whole incident, we'd love to hear your thoughts on the sentencing of the marathon bomber today."

On the other end of the line I sat there stunned. They had sentenced the marathon bomber today and I had no idea. I still call that terrorist "the marathon bomber" because I refuse to give him the recognition and acknowledgment of saying his real name. It was something I began as soon as he was identified as the perpetrator and have maintained to this day.

My eyes gazed out at the beauty before me, a vast canyon with stark rock formations and the dense bush below, all laying below a crystal-clear blue sky. I was so small. I felt so small. Over the past few hours I had reached a peace, both with running and within myself that I had not had in years, but now the marathon bombing was crashing back in to my peripheral vision. As I sat on that hill, salty and muddy and overwhelmed, I began to realize that it would never go away. That day, those events, the trauma of the thoughts I experienced before reuniting with my family, they would always be a part of me now. So how would I deal with it?

In that moment, faced with what could have been a crushing realization, I made the conscious decision to accept it. The marathon bombing will always be a part of me, but it does not have to define me.

The long pause was broken by the reporter. "Ey, um, ya there mate? You, uh, I'm guessing you didn't know about this?" He began to sound uncomfortable now.

"I had absolutely no idea. Haven't really had much TV the past couple of weeks."

He definitely sounded uncomfortable now.

"Oh, well, they actually made the announcement of the decision while you were running this morning. They sentenced him to death. What do you think, Bobby?" he nervously asked.

I talked about how I don't believe it is right to put him to death because it is the easy way out. A life of confinement is a far worse punishment than ending it all for him. Taking his life would never achieve closure or justice for the atrocities that he committed. The fact of the matter was that it was no longer important to me. Sure, I held an opinion of what I thought would be best, but the only thing that could ever truly bother me is if they let him go free. This was about me now. I was taking the focus away from the torment the past had caused me, and was instead looking at how it could inspire me.

After multiple thank yous, the journalist hung up the phone and I hobbled back to the hostel for a shower to freshen up before dinner. Sitting still on the grass for so long had drastically cooled my body temperature and I craved a warm shower. Stripping out of my muddy clothes, I made my way to the communal shower only to be greeted by cold water from the leaky nozzle. I literally could not tolerate the chill in my fragile state, so I just turned the shower off and put a clean set of clothes on over my dirty body.

Hopefully I would be able to take a shower once I arrived at Brenda's house for dinner. I was due to meet her in just over an hour when she would pick me up and bring me to her home for the generous reward of a home-cooked meal. At the very least, I had put some clean clothes on and organized my pack before heading to our meeting point. Brenda pulled up next to me and waved me into the car.

"So nice to finally meet you, dear!" She smiled at me, a motherly tone to her voice. It was really comforting.

"Brenda, I'm so sorry I smell awful." I had to get that obvious statement out of the way because I was so self-conscious. "They only had cold water in the showers, and I was freezing. I just couldn't—"

She cut me off. "No bother! We'll get you all sorted! You must be so exhausted. Home's only a short drive now, you can wash up while I finish dinner."

The shower was heavenly. It was the first "nice" bathroom I had been in since leaving the U.S.; it had a mosaic tiled floor and even a towel rack. The steaming water washed the caked mud from my body and soothed my aching muscles. I stepped out to find a warm, plush towel waiting for me.

When I walked out of the bathroom, I was greeted by a dog, her two children, and husband in the quaint living room of her beautiful home. On top of that a magnificent smell filled the air, wafting into the dining room from the kitchen.

Brenda made me one of the greatest post-race meals I have ever had: a roast lamb, Aussie style, with all the fixings. We all sat at the table as she joked about being my Australian mom after I told her how grateful my own mother was that she was having me for dinner. I answered all of her children's questions about America, and in turn queried her husband, who also worked as a guide, about adventures in the Australian bush.

After we finished eating she generously offered to house me for the night, but I told her I needed to return to watch Kevin finish the one hundred-kilometer race. I thanked her for the dinner, the hospitality, and for doing the story on me, handing her a paramedic pin as a keepsake. I waved bye to the kids and her husband drove me back to race headquarters.

The air was dark and cold but I will never forget the smile on Kevin's face as he crossed the late night finish line, Ian and myself both waiting to greet him. We all hugged him, and then were quickly off to collapse in our narrow bunks, falling to sleep even more effortlessly than the night before.

My news story ran in the *Sydney Morning Herald* the next day to the grand approval of many of my Aussie friends who shared it on Facebook. I thought it was cool to be in international news and began to read some of the comments on the SMH Facebook page about the article. There was a lot of positive support, but I was shocked to find that I was also heavily criticized. I was called a "tosser" and a "wanker," both of which required translations from my foreign friends. Although I was deeply offended by some of the comments, it quickly taught me my first lesson on being in the public eye: people are not always going to like you.

That's just the way it is, and over time, the more newspaper articles and stories I've been interviewed for, the better I've learned to ignore it and shake it off. Despite this knowledge, there will be times when one stupid comment will eat away at me, the frustration always more directed at myself for letting it bother me.

My train leaving the Blue Mountains departed early the next morning, and it was time to say bye to my new friends. When it came to say bye to Kevin, he extended an invite for me to stay with him in Christchurch, as I would be passing through there in two weeks' time. I thanked him for the offer and we connected on Facebook to coordinate a plan.

• • •

Australia had depleted much of my bank account and I was excited to be moving on to New Zealand. As someone new to traveling, I had diligently prepaid for many of the excursions and hostel rooms. This revealed itself as a strategy with both positive and negative aspects, and the experience certainly helped shape my future travels. It was nice to have a plan, but I found it often restricted me. As I met more and more people and heard about their experiences on the road, I would have loved the flexibility to change my plans, but I was locked in. The only real benefit was that I had prepaid a vast amount of the major expenses, taking away some of the financial worries.

So I flew into Auckland and tried my hand at bungy jumping. I bussed around the North Island and stopped by Hobbitton, a necessity for any massive *Lord of the Rings* nerd. The majority of my time in New Zealand, however, was spent exploring the incredible beauty of the South Island, which totally blew my expectations out the water. Consequently, feeling that there was so much to do and see, with so little time, I elected to keep moving and not deviate from my plan. I messaged Kevin to say I couldn't stop by, and that I'd see him next time. After all I had seen in New Zealand so far, I knew for sure that I would be back.

Just like that, my first big solo trip had come to an end. Before I knew it I was on an incredibly long plane ride back to the United States;

fulfilled, satisfied, and inspired for the next adventure. I knew for sure that through running in these remote places I would continue to heal.

Out of the many lessons I learned from this first adventure on my own, the saddest came about a month after I returned home. While browsing Facebook during my morning breakfast, I began to see many condolence messages in my newsfeed. Kevin Foyle, my Kiwi ultra-runner buddy, had passed away suddenly. An incredibly healthy and skilled athlete in his early fifties was now suddenly dead. I was left kicking myself that I declined his offer to visit him in Christchurch, forgoing the opportunity to spend more time running the hills with him.

The morning after I heard of Kevin's death, I took a black Sharpie and drew a capital K on the mesh toe of my neon green Adidas running shoes. Then I went out for a long, long run, saying goodbye to Kevin in the only way I could see fit.

In the weeks following I reflected a lot on my decision to not go to Christchurch. I had naively just assumed I could return to New Zealand at any time to visit and run with him. Now I never will. Too often in life do we say, "There's always time," or "I'll get to it." The truth is, life is incredibly fragile, and it's immensely important to seize the opportunities in front of you. Initially I was both sad and pissed off that I declined Kevin's offer. I am now able to be thankful for the profound role that this event has played in my life, revealing to me, in the most raw way, the importance of making the most of every day and every opportunity.

Moving forward, I was not going to be so rigid with my travel plans. I needed to allow flexibility for those spontaneous and serendipitous encounters that inevitably occur through the course of an adventure. Although it is nice, and it is comfortable, to follow a routine and preplanned schedule, it's restrictive and inhibits the ability to diverge.

We love comfort. Human nature is to gravitate towards the easiest option. It seems counterintuitive to leave our comfort zone, but when we do, and we step into a new place with a new plan and new people, that is when the true adventure begins. There is a world of truth in

Eleanor Roosevelt's classic quote, "Do one thing every day that scares you." Without challenging ourselves we limit our ability for expansion and growth. All of my favorite and most impactful memories resulted from an event I didn't plan for. From then on, it became a priority to have minimal structure or planning to constrain my trips, allowing the possibility of real adventure.

Time is finite for us. Traveling more while I have my health and means to do so seems like the most logical thing to me. Personally, I felt that I had made considerable progress in rectifying my emotional turmoil by running in remote Australia, despite the realization that I would never outrun the presence of the marathon bombing in my life Once removed from the chaos of urban environments, I felt able to experience running in its most pure and beautiful form. Connecting with myself in this way, in wild and magnificent places, truly felt like the best medicine for my still recovering mind. If this was the case, then there were certainly ample opportunities to run races like this all over the world. In my mind, the best way to ensure I was always moving forward was to make things goal-oriented. It was this that brought me to the biggest challenge I had set for myself thus far: to run a marathon on all seven continents.

CHAPTER FIVE

FROZEN FEET

King George Island, Antarctica
January 2016

Summer passed by and I entered my final year of college feeling invigorated by my recent trip to Australia. I was riding a high from the adventure, full of hope that I had discovered the cure to "fix myself." As the days and weeks passed by, that feeling slowly faded, leaving a vacuum that seemed to breed apathy and restlessness. Some will know and name that feeling as post-travel depression.

Fortunately, I found some solace running and trekking through the stark and beautiful White Mountains right on my doorstep in New Hampshire. Almost every day I was not working, I would train on these beautiful trails and summits. Thankfully, many of the people in my life also had a love for those mountains. I'd frequently find myself getting lost in the woods with people like Rachel, Shaina, Dave, or Jim. All people who had spent years exploring the Whites and were keen to show me everything they had to offer.

We all worked together in the emergency room, but spent just as much time together outside of the hospital. Rachel was one of the nurses, and we developed a special connection because she had also deviated from the 'traditional path', spending much of her twenties traveling and road tripping around the United States with her husband. She validated my decisions and encouraged my wanderlust, dissipating the negativity I sometimes faced from other people in my life. Rachel also understood how special the mountains were for our mental health, and I found myself sharing some of the darkness I still struggled with from the marathon bombing.

Healing from such a traumatic event does not follow a linear path; rather it is a rollercoaster of ups and downs, elations and failures along the way. Even following the recovery process I had started in Australia, I feared to test how well I was doing. Feeling a bit of a coward, I did my best to avoid Boston that summer and continued to hide in the mountains. I was afraid that my progress was all just an illusion. An exciting but temporary elation brought on by the introduction of traveling as a new passion in my life. If that was the case, I knew I needed to continue to 'be distracted'; I craved to move onwards to the next continent on my recently created mission. Unfortunately, that meant waiting until winter because the continent I had chosen was one where there weren't many options for races at all. Being one of the most logistically difficult races to arrange was a great distraction, and the thought of pulling it off sustained me through the second half of that year. I counted down the days 'til I could realize my fantastical plan. I was heading to Antarctica.

● ● ●

When I first signed up for the White Continent Marathon it still seemed like an intangible goal. Even after I sent the entry payments and purchased my cold weather running gear, I didn't believe this journey would actually happen until I physically boarded the plane to the first meeting point in Chile. It was a cold January afternoon when my parents and Nana B picked me up at school in New Hampshire to drive me down to Logan Airport in Boston.

The ride went incredibly fast, so many ideas racing around my head about the adventure I would soon embark on. I was struggling through an IT band injury that began nagging right before Christmas, but the usual "anxious runner syndrome" did not plague me. This race was not about a time goal or setting a new personal best, this was to return to that Australian mentality of traveling on land mostly untainted by man. Rediscovering the exhilarating pulse of running through engaging terrain and to experience the sport at its primitive roots.

My mother sat anxiously in the backseat of the car, dreading the thought of me leaving again. These adventures were beginning to wear on her, and I did feel bad. Nana B, my "biggest fan" along with my mom, sat beside her and tried to comfort her in a motherly fashion. Being an only child definitely has its pros and cons, but I always feel a little guilty each time I leave my mom because of it.

My attempt at a joke about smuggling home a penguin earned a brief smile from the corner of her mouth. If it were up to her, I think that car ride would have lasted forever. Every day I am reminded how lucky I am to have parents that care so deeply but are also exceptionally supportive of my dreams.

Pulling up to the curb outside the terminal, my dad opened the door to help me with my bag. There is constantly a sense of urgency at Logan Airport. State police are ever present, facilitating the flow of traffic at a brisk pace. Goodbyes are always rushed, sometimes a blessing in disguise as you are hurried away from dwelling on the sadness of it.

My mom wrapped me up in a big hug, told me to be careful, have fun, and how much she loved me. Then she told me to be careful one more time. Nana B did the same. My dad pulled me into a tight embrace, his round belly bouncing off of me. "Have the time of your life," he said. "And be careful about the shrinkage!" he yelled, closing the car door with a big smirk on his face.

"Bob!" my mom yelled as she gave me one more hug; she always had to be the last person to hug me before I left. Once in the car she turned out the window and waved, mouthing "I love you" as they pulled away. Anyone watching this exchange could have mistaken my two-week jaunt to the bottom of the world for a year-long perilous journey.

The next few hours went by slowly as I checked and rechecked my watch, just itching to get up in the air. Travel can be heavily glamourized, Instagram and social media accounts enticing people to leave home for the "glory shot." Everyone desires to travel to see the ocean sunsets, gushing waterfalls, and magnificent wildlife. Those who are actually fortunate enough to gallivant with a backpack around foreign lands know that this is only a fraction of how your time is spent—a literal snapshot into your adventure. Time alone on buses and trains, long layovers, sleeping on airport floors, and crappy meals with stale bread and unidentifiable fruits are much more common. Money disappears quickly when you're away from home so "tourist traps" aren't an option for entertainment, but this enables better memories to be made.

My favorite moments from my adventures are the simplest. I would take a bottle of cheap rum on a beach with new friends over a Sydney Opera House show ten times out of ten.

These memories and experiences of my brief traveling career made waiting on the floor of Miami International Airport four hours later, munching on a can of Pringles, tolerable, and even enjoyable. Everything in life really is all about perspective.

The red eye to Santiago, Chile brought much needed sleep and a stiff neck when I woke up thousands of miles from where I started. I viewed the sunrise that morning in a different hemisphere from which I saw it set. I looked out the window to catch a glimpse of the Andes dotting the gorgeous landscape below. Adventure surged through my veins and my eyes closed to salvage a bit more sleep.

Two short connecting flights brought me to the quaint little city of Punta Arenas. This small port hub on the south Chilean coast was our "staging area" where we would await a much-anticipated flight to Antarctica in a couple of days' time.

I retrieved my pack from a baggage claim area a fraction the size of airports in the States, and made my way out into the warm South American sun. Although winter was fairly mild in New England this year, the seventy-degree weather was a welcome upgrade as the sun hit my pasty skin.

There would be time later to enjoy my first January summer in the southern hemisphere, but for now I had another task at hand. The hotel where I was meeting the group from Marathon Adventures, the company organizing this race, was roughly twenty kilometers from the airport. Flagging a taxi would be fairly easy, but communicating directions in my broken Spanish would prove slightly more challenging.

This was a matter of pride for me. Whenever I traveled to Spanish speaking countries, I would always do my best to converse with locals without using English or visual cues. The more time I spent in South and Central America, the easier it became, but my goal of fluency still loomed very far in the future.

My enthusiastic cab driver greeted me with a hearty pat on the back. "¡Amigo! ¿A dónde vamos?" he exclaimed as he motioned me to put my bag in the back of his weathered Toyota Camry. My heavy pack hit the worn cloth seat with a muted *thud*.

I would always panic speaking Spanish after I hadn't practiced in another country for a while. My last adventure that required language skills was in Honduras ten months prior, when the most important and frequently used word was "cerveza." When I panic in these situations, I always start with "hola," no matter what.

"¡Hola!" I almost yelled, in a cracked voice. Thirteen hours of travel had left my mouth dry and my tongue unloosened from the absence of use. I cleared my throat and processed what I wanted to say in my mind. "¿Puedes conducirme a este hotel?" I caved and motioned to the hotel picture on my phone, asking him to take me to "this one." The rust was certainly alive and well on that part of my hippocampus.

"¡Ah por supuesto!" He smiled and ran around to the passenger seat to open the door for me. *At least we were on the same page,* I thought, and smiled back at his incredible politeness. I nestled my smaller backpack between my legs and looked for my seatbelt, which was not present. *No worries,* I thought as I glanced up at the large crack in the windshield. The engine roared and we were on our way.

Twenty-five minutes of confusing conversation, awkward pauses, and half-hearted laughs brought us to the front drive of the hotel. The charismatic driver removed my bag from the back and I gave him a big, enthusiastic handshake along with a generous tip. He flashed a larger smile and sped off, leaving me to meet up with the rest of the Marathon Adventures group.

This was the first time I had ever booked a trip through a "marathon travel company," but options become pretty limited when you start looking for a race in Antarctica. However, I cannot say enough about the professionalism and enthusiasm provided by Steve Hibbs and the crew at Marathon Adventures. After months of corresponding by email, Steve even ended up being one of the first people to greet me in the hotel lobby.

After checking in with the woman at the front desk (in English), I saw a trio of people gathered by the elevators with bulky bags and brightly colored jackets, large Antarctica patches decorating their backs. I quickly scooted over to them and Steve introduced me to the two other members of his team, Adam and Whitney. Their energy and excitement was obvious and I fed off it immediately. It was the same type of sensation I experience at most races, the one that runners involuntarily bring with them everywhere they go, and synergizes when they come together.

After the introductions they informed me of a briefing for runners being held tomorrow night that would explain the tentative itinerary for the trip. They also invited me on a training run the next morning to which I happily obliged.

I asked them if my roommate had arrived yet and was disappointed to learn his flights had been delayed so he would now not be arriving until tomorrow evening. I had been looking forward to meeting the friendly German that I had been talking to through Facebook since our room assignments were posted by Steve a few weeks prior.

I retired to my room and took full advantage of the free Wi-Fi to contact my parents and let them know I had arrived safely. The "perks" of booking this race through a company were starting to become very obvious. I was not in a dirty hostel with no temperature control and an army of insects, but rather a clean hotel room furnished with immaculate (kind of) bedding and air conditioning. My bank account on the other hand felt significantly less comfort from this luxury. Although it was nice, it did take away from my pride in feeling adventurous, but I was not one to complain while I lounged in my soft bed in a wonderfully air-conditioned room before quickly falling asleep.

My iPhone alarm buzzed loudly on the nightstand as seven a.m. arrived faster than I had hoped. Luckily, there was not much of a time change from home so my body felt relatively normal as I slid off my boxers and into my running shorts. *Running shorts in January*? I thought. *This is pretty damn awesome.* Since my running career began, the month of January was consistently a brutal gauntlet of blizzards and cold spells that became a necessary evil when training for the Boston Marathon. At this time of year my shorts were usually buried under all my thermal gear in the depths of my dresser.

I met the three peppy team leaders from yesterday in the lobby of the hotel, casually stretching while they chatted, that subconscious habit innate to runners everywhere. They gave me a quick hello and told me we were waiting for one more to join us on the warm-up run. As the conversation went on I learned that we would be running the Punta

Arenas Marathon course with Steve as he mapped out the distances.

The group Marathon Adventures offers this second marathon during the Antarctica trip specifically as a bonus for those trying to complete a seven continent marathon challenge. Essentially, you have two marathons in a span of a couple days, but this gives you the ability to complete almost a third of the continent goal, which is very appealing from a marketing perspective.

Because I was recovering from an injury, it was my hope that the White Continent Marathon would be held first. Since completing a marathon on Antarctica is logistically much more difficult than in South America, I did not want to injure myself further trying to run in Punta Arenas. To be honest, I wasn't sure I really wanted to run that one at all. It almost felt like cheating to me, not in the sense that it's not a real marathon, but a "staged" race in a city was not what I was looking for when I set out to run in the most remote places around the world.

What determines the timeline and order of the races is the weather of King George Island, Antarctica. This small piece of rocky land off the Antarctic Peninsula hosted the White Continent Marathon each year and has no formal airport. For a plane to land, there needs to be roughly 500 meters of clear "runway" on the gravel that packed part of the coastline. Any snow, ice, or excessive wind speeds would prevent a safe landing for the plane we would be taking across the frozen sea.

This makes the trip a waiting game. Weather reports are checked religiously every hour by pilots and the race organizers, constantly seeking the first opportunity for a flight window. Steve informed me that they would give the first update tonight at the group meeting and pasta dinner as to what it was looking like for our race dates.

A short Indian man with long hair, a beard, and dressed in typical running swag walked over from the elevators, clearly the fifth member of our training session.

"Hey guys!" he said cheerfully. He had met the others yesterday when he had arrived, but offered out a hand to me and introduced himself as Sandy. We quickly walked and talked our way to the door, all very eager to get our legs moving, stir crazy from the long flights the previous day.

We set off at a fairly light pace on a nice sidewalk route along the coast, sparkling ocean and fishing boats dotting the horizon. At first, I just listened to the chatter amongst the group of very well-traveled runners. It was a treat listening to all the running stories, hearing about races previously unknown to me that sounded purely magical. I was taking mental notes while Sandy spoke of his experience at the Mt. Kilimanjaro Marathon last year when suddenly a small commotion in the water caught my eye. "Look!" I shouted, clearly more excited than I should've been.

Everyone turned just in time to see a perfectly undisturbed ocean surface. Rescuing me from embarrassment, Steve commented that they routinely see dolphins jumping and spinning out of the water along this route, keeping your eyes hopefully out to sea was a nice running distraction. Sure enough we were treated to a spinning show by a gorgeous dolphin just a mile further down the road.

Steve would pause every so often to mark the sidewalk for distance and turn-around points for the marathon and fifty-kilometer race. The course was a little more than five kilometers out and five kilometers back, completed four times to add up to your marathon distance.

This made the race even less appealing to me and I began to think about skipping it entirely to focus solely on Antarctica. A four-loop course on a city sidewalk was not why I wanted to run the continents, but the appeal of having completed four total continents by the end of this trip was also extraordinarily tempting. *It will be a game-time decision*, I told myself as we ran back towards the hotel from the turnaround point.

Tales of races in far-off lands filled the rest of the run and before I knew it, I began to recognize the street art painted on the buildings next to our hotel. Running with a group certainly makes the time fly by, which is enjoyable in its own sense, but very different to the solidarity offered by the trails.

Luckily, all of this distracted me from my nagging IT band and the run was virtually pain-free. This again swayed the pendulum and made me cautiously optimistic about the idea of something I had never attempted before: two marathons in one week.

Back at the hotel, I prepared for the first meet and greet with the rest of the adventurous bunch of runners that had their sights set on running on Antarctica. After the nice sampling of stories I had listened to from Steve, Adam, Sandy, and Whitney, I was eager to be inspired further. Tonight also happened to be the AFC Championship game between the Patriots and Broncos and for the first time I would listen to a broadcaster call the American football game in Spanish. So I diligently put on my Tom Brady jersey and made my way downstairs. I met a whole slew of other runners at the hotel bar, all of which were excited Americans gathered around the TV, and most of them fans from Colorado. We exchanged playful jabs back and forth until Steve called us in for the meeting, just before halftime.

Two long tables split the middle of the banquet room and were set up with pasta, bread, salads, drinks, and anything a group of hungry and overly tired runners could hope for. I took a seat near the end of the second table where I met my roommate Matthias. After an extraordinary headache of flight changes and delays, he finally made it from his home in Germany to Punta Arenas late this afternoon, and I'm very glad he did.

Matthias is truly one of the nicest and most genuine humans I have met in my travels. We chatted about many things ranging from his studies back home, to travel, and of course, running. Antarctica would be the seventh continent for Matthias, and I couldn't imagine what a spectacular feeling that had to be. I congratulated him in advance and he began to tell me his story.

When I asked what races he had done on the other continents, he told me that he "hadn't really done races" and he could quickly tell I was perplexed by the look on my face. He began running just to be healthy and push his body to test his limits. One day on a whim he went out and ran for forty-two kilometers back in Germany, his first marathon. But there was no finish line, no medal, no fans or race photographers, just the self-satisfaction of accomplishment. Matthias would continue to repeat this distance while he traveled the world between his years of university study, until he realized that he ran a marathon on every continent except for Antarctica. Now, it was time for him to finish this incredible goal. My new German friend was running the continents for the most important reason there is in the sport—the pure enjoyment of running as an entity in and of itself.

Don't get me wrong, I had enjoyed the big city races just as much as everyone else in the marathon-running community. That's what got me hooked on running to begin with. The incredible energy of the spectators and "celebrity feeling" of being an athlete inside the ropes is exhilarating. I think that many runners can get hung up on this aspect, and may lose sight of what is truly important. Everyone has their own reason for why they run and what makes them happy in the sport, and for a long time that was what did it for me in running. I wasn't running for myself though, it was all about how other people perceived me, and how tangible achievements made me feel successful, not how the sport did that on its own. Matthias had never fallen into that trap, and this made me respect him greatly.

This reflection on Matthias' experience also made me realize how I had changed as a runner since my obsession over the Boston Marathon jacket began so many years ago. Now it was about finding meaning in running, and getting far, far away from the crowds, to be with my own thoughts, and to heal. My experience in Australia, my training in the White Mountains of New Hampshire, and this upcoming marathon on one of the harshest and most isolated continents on the planet were all key components to my running evolution. Each time my brain, heart, and soul experienced one of these magical adventures on the trails, it healed the damage done by the Boston Marathon tragedy. And each time I grew stronger, so did my belief that running had transcended its original and seemingly shallow place in my life.

The dinner went by quickly as myself and some of the other runners were anxious to return to the football game. Steve and his staff gave a thoroughly detailed presentation on exactly what to expect for the week ahead. Unfortunately, the weather early on was looking dodgy at best and the White Continent Marathon would not be held at the start of the trip like I had hoped. Because of this, the Punta Arenas Marathon would be held tomorrow. Even though all of us had trained for months and were pretty experienced runners, it is still a shock to your system when you need to prepare yourself to run a marathon with less than twenty-four hours' notice.

In a mirror image of Australia, it was contrary to what I expected when I fell asleep swiftly and soundly that night, waking the next morning to the sound of Matthias getting ready. I guess it was time to make that game-time decision on whether or not to compete in this race.

I stretched my legs out on the bed and everything felt well-rested and ready to go with not even a minor protest from my IT band. With that, I chowed down on a Clif Bar and lazily tossed my running gear on, leaving my bag in disarray on the ground, a lazy luxury I would never have dreamed of in a hostel.

Matthias and I walked over to the makeshift start line, directly across the street from the vestibule of the hotel entrance. The salt air and stiff breeze were a welcome wake-up call to my still-sleepy brain. Marathon Adventures being an American-based tour group, the U.S. national anthem was played slightly incongruously through a phone speaker and the race began promptly after.

This was the smallest field I had ever ran in for a marathon, so I found myself in unfamiliar territory running with the lead pack. Chatting casually with some of the other guys up front for a bit, I enjoyed these first few miles getting to know some of my new friends. I imagined this was extremely different than what you could expect at the larger races, in the sense that we really weren't competing against each other. We were all just out on the course with the same goal: to complete a marathon in South America. That created an interesting atmosphere because even though I have always found runners to be very supportive of each other, it was even more amplified on this trip. Every single person wanted to see the whole group get to the finish line, and we would continue to wait no matter how long it took that last finisher.

I fell into my own groove after the first ten-kilometer loop and was pretty stoked on my pace and that my legs weren't feeling any ramifications from my nagging injuries. The second loop went by even quicker. The third loop, however, began to slow me down. The course brought us by a few warehouses where large commercial shipping vessels were docked for stock and repair. There also must have been some factories nearby because my nose cringed like industrialization was punching me in the face. This was not the South American marathon experience I wanted. I vowed that even after this race I *needed* to come back to this continent to run a true trail race in one of the incredibly beautiful landscapes this part of the world has to offer.

My watch interrupted my thoughts as it beeped, alerting me that twenty miles had passed. Simultaneously, I heard a yell in my direction coming from the road. My brain, conditioned from the marathon bombing, was immediately on high alert.

People were yelling to me and waving their arms from a car in oncoming traffic. I wasn't sure if I was about to be robbed, kidnapped, or both. Without trying to draw too much attention, I quickened my pace and began to look for a large group of people or an exit point, but I could find none. My heart was now pounding out of my chest; I could not believe I would be so unlucky to have another race interrupted by some horrific ending. How could I get out of here?

It's a funny feeling when you are faced with a version of yourself that you have tried to deny. In this case, my new reality was that I was suffering from Post Traumatic Stress Disorder (PTSD). It is a condition which always starts with a traumatic trigger; an event causing death or posing extreme threat to yourself or others. The DSM (Diagnostic and Statistical Manual of Mental Disorders) criteria describes this is as causing "intense fear, helplessness, or horror." It did not take long after the marathon bombing for me to start discovering the multitude of creative ways your mind finds to take you back to those moments of terror. A major one for me was my dreams—a cruel trick played when you should feel most secure from the world. But then there were also the physical manifestations of fear that plagued my day-to-day life: loud noises would make my heart race out of proportion, unattended bags caused me to break into a cold sweat, and unanswered phone calls brought on a panic that would cripple me. Despite, or maybe because of, this classic presentation of PTSD I did not accept the diagnosis; I refused it. I avoided this clinical way of defining my problems because then it would be admitting just that—that I had a problem. I felt that by avoiding this label I had a shield protecting me from the unwanted sympathy and attention that would follow those four letters. Sometimes it hurts even more when people treat you like you are broken. The difficulty to acknowledge that I wasn't okay weighed on me heavily, a dark secret that stopped me from truly opening up to even those closest to me. Regardless, it was events like this, on the side of the road in Punta Arenas, Chile, that reminded me of the undeniable issues that continued to torment my brain, whether I chose to accept them or not.

The car got closer and pulled off to the side of the road right in front of me. Now I truly thought that I was done for, dread pulling on every cell in my body. A man poked out his head from the backseat window and pointed to me.

"Bobby!" he yelled. I squinted my eyes and recognized him as one of the runners from the meeting last night. My head spun with relief, but also obviously a good deal of confusion.

"Get in!" he screamed out to me. Again the feeling that something had gone horribly wrong seeped into my veins, nausea filling my mouth. With my attitude and instincts jaded by the Boston Marathon bombing, my amygdala changed gears into full panic and I felt myself freeze up.

I did not hear an explosion. I could not see any smoke. Regardless, every fiber of my being was preparing myself for another bombing.

"Get in! Come on! Hurry up! We got a flight!" A big smile came across his face as the last words slipped excitedly from his mouth.

Still dazed, I opened the back door to what I now recognized as a taxi with three other runners in the occupied seats. Then it all clicked, but it took someone else saying it for me to actually believe the news.

"The weather cleared! We need to get back now, you've got half an hour to pack. Everyone else is at the hotel already. We're going to Antarctica my friend!" He clapped his hands loudly and high-fived one of the other guys in the backseat triumphantly.

I smiled, but my system was still in shock. I went from being twenty miles into a marathon, to thinking there had been a terror attack, to finding out we were leaving for Antarctica within the hour, all in a span of five minutes. As the car pulled up to the front of the hotel we all scuttled out and went to our rooms, my mind still dissociated from the reality unfolding around me.

When I hastily opened the door to our room, Matthias was almost done packing already. Conversely, I looked at my bag and immediately regretted leaving it in such a disheveled state this morning. Bathing suits covered wool socks, water bottles were jammed under cell phone chargers—it was a mess. Doing as best I could and praying I hadn't forgotten anything, everything was jammed into my pack and within ten minutes we were out the door.

The bus ride to the airport was filled with excited chatter and also disgruntled remarks from many upset people that were pulled off the marathon course. Yes it sucked, but Steve had to make that call. How could he not? We got a flight opening to Antarctica on the first day of our window; that was incredibly lucky and hardly ever happens.

As we got to the airport, most people were too excited to care anymore anyway. We had our own little terminal in the already tiny airport so everyone was huddled close together with bags strewn in every direction. Within the hour, we were in the plane and up in the air, on our way to somewhere I had dreamed of going for so many years, before I had ever thought to run a marathon.

Hunger was destroying my stomach, and my legs were increasingly stiff and sore, but these distracting factors barely registered as my giddy mind contemplated the amazing adventure ahead. Antarctic related reading material in the back pocket of the seat in front of me made the flight pass quickly. The story of Shackleton's Antarctic expedition completely captured all of my attention until the man next to me tapped my shoulder and pointed out the window.

My eyes darted over just in time to see the magnificent beauty of a stark white iceberg contrast against the dark blue freezing water below. More and more icebergs popped up below us as we approached the coastline. Antarctica was right there, I was viewing it not through a computer screen or *National Geographic* article, but with my very own eyes.

The pilot touched down with a rough jolt onto the packed gravel "runway" just over the jagged ice peaks on the coast and slowed to a bumpy but not nauseating stop. Every single person on that plane had the exact same wide-eyed glowing smile. Dreams were about to come true.

All bundled up in anticipation of the harsh climate to come, we waddled, in a similar fashion to our future penguin friends, to the exit at the front of the plane. As soon as I poked my head out the door the cold bit harshly at my exposed face, the wind unforgivingly lashed at my clothes, and a dark sky loomed threateningly above. I could not have been more excited about it. This is what adventure feels like.

We hiked up a snow-covered gravel path in the bitter chill to a small research station where the scientists-turned-rugged-survivalists greeted us with warm smiles and firm handshakes. The relief from the howling winds was welcomed along with a much-needed bathroom break, which ended up being the only one we would use indoors while on the continent.

Continuing on down the rocky path in the direction of the coast, frost coated my eyelashes as routinely as pollen would on a spring day in New England. The crunch of the crisp snow underfoot evoked a nostalgic feeling of winters at home.

Our campsite came into view around the bend, a wide plateau with enough space for the sixteen or so three-person tents plus one larger tent staged for food and supplies with an adjacent toilet system. The bright yellow, high visibility four-season tents dotted the horizon and grew larger as we approached.

Leave no trace was in full effect on King George Island, as it should be in a place so pure and pristine. This involved peeing into a funnel connected to specialized waste drums and pooping into bio-conservative waste bags to be disposed of appropriately. The thin canvas walls of the bathroom were not the most comforting while dropping your pants in a stiff Antarctic wind, but any shelter was better than none.

It was now six p.m. and the sun still shone high in the sky, giving a brilliant glow of orange which kissed the clouds, softening the dramatic starkness of the barren landscape. The sun would remain guard from above late into the night, until a brief window of darkness took the last light from our shivering bodies.

Since the weather had cleared, we spent hours exploring the surrounding terrain, making the most of the brief time we would get to enjoy this fantastic icy wonderland. My watch brought me back to reality when the display informed me it was midnight, four and a half hours 'til the race start. After running over twenty miles, frantically rushing onto a plane, and making it to this frozen tundra, I theoretically should have been out like a light. A combination of nervous excitement and cold bones prevented sleep from overtaking me too easily. The wind howled as I snuggled into the edge of our three-person tent. The gusts whipped the nylon siding against the top of my head with a loud "smack." Wedged into my sleeping bag with five layers on top, five on bottom, a beanie, and two pairs of wool socks, I drifted off, praying I wouldn't have to leave my warm sleeping bag in the middle of the night to pee.

When Steve finally woke us in the wee hours of the morning, the sun was already high in the sky. Given the wonky sleep schedule and chaos of the previous days, I could have been convinced without blinking an eye that it was midday.

A light breakfast accompanied by nervous chatter among my fellow runners set the mood for the day. There was absolutely nobody who was not excited to be there. Talk, from finishing times to how many penguins we would see, ricocheted amongst us in our prerace conversations. The steam from the hot tea blended naturally with the mist of our breath in the cold morning air. Then Steve finally called that it was time to officially begin the race.

We lined up on the gravel road created by the resident researchers and gazed off to the mountains and snow-covered plains. A simple "Go!" set us off and I once again took off with the "lead pack" of four guys at a light jog up the initial incline. The run course itself was four six-mile "figure-eight" style loops that resulted in passing through "base camp" eight times before the finish. This detail would turn out to be an extremely valuable asset when I realized less than a mile into the race that I was severely over-layered. Within the first mile, sweat soaked every inch of my body. Today was much more mild than the previous night, causing wardrobe confusion for most of the athletes who, shockingly, had zero experience running in the climate of Antarctica. When anyone asks about the marathon in Antarctica, I feel like I am disappointing them when I describe the weather. I did not lose any digits or have my eyes freeze shut in a cataclysmic storm. Even though the wind was strong, temperatures rested in the fifteen to twenty-degree Fahrenheit range; training during winter in New England is often colder than this.

I ditched my heavier shell at the first crossing back through camp, which was initially a welcome relief to my saturated body, but this tactic quickly backfired. The layer underneath was still soaking wet and began to freeze in the brisk and unforgiving air. Taking an optimistic outlook on this, at least I could actually tell people that I froze in Antarctica. I relied on body heat to warm my clothes as I increased the cadence of my stride, now heading downhill towards the coast.

My first glimpse of the ocean dotted with icebergs and framed by massive glaciers is eternally saved in my memory as true and pristine beauty in nature. It was at that moment it truly hit home how incredible it was to be standing in this spot and breathing this air. Antarctica is one of the few places left on our beautiful planet with an almost negligible human footprint. The excitement of that thought increased my pace, my legs keen to explore more of the real-life utopia before me. It soon became apparent that the majority of the race's spectators were situated along the rocky shoreline, squawking away loudly. A trio of chinstrap penguins, a cluster of Adélie penguins, and a pair of chubby sea lions looked on at the strange two-legged creatures bounding through their territory. Well, the sea lions couldn't have cared less, but the penguins were another story. With very minimal human interference in their daily lives, they were curious about the bizarre newcomers in colorful attire. The result was a game of dodging and weaving around the penguins that would continuously waddle onto the track that made up the course near the beach.

Adorable penguins on a running path of fresh snow, sea lion barks that filled the air, and a backdrop of steel blue translucent icebergs dotting a frigid bay created a perpetual winter running wonderland.

Proceeding along the course, my feet fought a constant battle of freezing, thawing, and refreezing. Ice crystals built up around the lime green mesh of my Adidas roadrunners. At this point, I had still not adapted my kit to trail running and was irresponsibly oblivious to my need for trail shoes at this early stage of my adventure-running career. Today, instead of the comfort of a tarmac sidewalk, they valiantly battled the thawing and freezing cycle thrown at them by their new environment. The moisture from the snow, slush, and occasional puddle would saturate the mesh siding of my shoes (and still two pairs of socks underneath). As the course wound its way back onto the gravel research roads and time was allowed for the shoes to dry, they would begin to freeze again in the arctic air. Scrunching my toes up would now cause a "crunch" from the breaking of newly formed ice crystals woven into the soft material. A smile crept across my face—where else in the world could this happen?

Approaching the middle of the course, the path became unclear as large fields of snow over the height of my head blocked the way. As I got closer, I noticed a winding path right through the middle of the monumental snow bank. Some of the local researchers, Chilean Navy personnel from the base on the island, and race directors, had shoveled and hammered down a path for us to run on. The ground was bumpy and uneven, sometimes causing a foot to penetrate straight through an extra couple inches, throwing you off-balance. Thankfully, there were steep walls on either side, and I frequently had to reach out and catch myself against the hard-packed borders of snow. This snow tunnel continued for a hundred meters or so until the course persisted on its typical trend of snow, ice, water, and gravel.

Marathons that are created by repeating loops are generally a punishment in a torturous cycle of monotony. Today however, running the same route multiple times was an absolute privilege. After the first loop, each twist and turn brought the same excitement at being able to continually gaze upon the bleak icebergs and run through the field of inquisitive penguins. By the time my tired, soaked feet crossed the finish line, I still wasn't ready to be done. Before changing into dry clothes, I walked over to my tent and unraveled a jacket encasing a precious sixteen-ounce can of Pabst Blue Ribbon. I made a promise to all the guys back home that I would carry our beloved beer all the way from New England to the southern-most continent. Handing my phone to race director Steve Hibbs, I made my way back to the finish line to shotgun the coldest beer of my entire life.

A range of emotions flooded my brain as I stripped the layers off my cold body once back in the tent, still buzzing from the race and the beer in my stomach. This marathon had felt unreachable when I first found out it existed, and the months of planning and saving had only served to make it feel further away. Yet now, despite the intense build up and anticipation, I truly felt I had had one of the greatest experiences of my life. Sometimes, when things in life are preceded by promises of the amazing experience they will deliver, they do not live up to the expectation, bringing disappointment to an experience that truly was fine. This is why I think expectations are a dangerous thing to possess in regards to traveling.

In one of Jason Silva's National Public Radio segments, he was discussing the conundrum of the "Instagram generation" in the modern world. One of the resounding quotes from his talk is that, "The Instagram generation experiences the present as an anticipated memory."

Basically, when traveling or attending an event, many people let social media dictate their experience before they go without them even realizing it. I'm guilty of it too. For example, I knew before I even finalized my plans to venture to Antarctica that I would see penguins, icebergs, and beautiful, dramatic landscapes. Therefore, I also knew that I would probably be posting pictures of penguins, icebergs, and dramatic landscapes.

What that does though, is creates this expectation of a place I have never been to before, and in a way preemptively dictates my experience for me. In addition, while I am there and in the moment, I am thinking about what my social media post will include, further affecting my present reality. Unfortunately, I feel that this detracts from the ability to experience something as it is and to the fullest. In the modern world, when a cell phone or camera is always in hand, this situation becomes ever harder to avoid.

Over time and after traveling more, I have made a conscious effort to avoid this. Simple things such as leaving my phone in the bottom of my bag, or snapping just a single picture for a second as opposed to getting hung up on capturing the perfect image, have helped. It's more important to me to have used my senses experiencing the beauty of the world than to be able to reflect back on it through a photograph at a later time. If I wanted to do the latter, I might as well see the world through the internet because then I'll be viewing better pictures than I could ever take anyway.

Despite any of this interference, this adventure had still more than exceeded my expectations. The race, and journey to it, was memorable, exhilarating, and beautiful. Even better, was that I still had a few remaining hours to luxuriously enjoy my time on one of the most stunning pieces of land I have ever stepped foot on.

It was either on the plane to Antarctica or in the hotel in Chile when another runner named Dave Wright and I made a pact to do a polar plunge while in Antarctica. We were already here, on one of the coldest places on the planet, and God only knows if we would ever make it back again. We had to make it count.

Right up until the moment we were stripping down on the rocky shore, as the bitter wind assaulted my exposed skin, I had half-hoped he had forgotten.

"You ready, buddy?" Dave smiled as he clapped his hand on my back.

"Ah, damn. Ready as I'm gonna be, man." We walked up from the shore to our campsite to grab our towels. Dave spun around quickly and walked back towards the boat.

Our audience consisted of a sleepy elephant seal snoring away in a noisy chorus, a group of Chilean Navy members snickering together in a circle, and a dozen or so other runners with GoPros and iPhones already recording. Looking out at the unforgiving yet serene water, a chinstrap penguin poked his head out above the surface. I was all ready to go while Dave debated on whether or not to take the plunge naked.

"Can you hurry up dude?" I yelled over to him, shivering and running my hands up and down my torso.

"Let's do it!" he yelled back, underwear still on.

We charged into the ocean and the thrill negated the sensation of the frigid water running up above my calves. We threw our hands up, yelled, and screamed, enjoying the pure moment of being wild. When we got further out we turned to each other, high-fived, and then fell backwards into the ocean. That's when the cold hit. When my head reemerged into the fresh Antarctic air, my whole body burned from the freezing cold water. We hustled back to shore to the cheers of our fellow racers, quickly handing us our towels. Within minutes my soaked hair had already frozen into icicles, but it was worth every second.

Dave and I gazed back out on the horizon and the same penguin popped back up where we had just been, probably confused beyond belief as to what the hell had just happened, interrupting his leisurely swim around the bay.

After seeing our display of bravado and stupidity, a Chilean Navy member who had watched from the shore laughed heartily and approached us and offered a little bit of an extra tour once we were back in dry clothes. Our little stunt seemed to have earned us some respect, or maybe it was sympathy, from the man we now knew as Nico.

In relatively speaking fresh and dry clothes, we climbed up a snowy hill, bringing us further and further above all the man-made structures in the area. The wind gusted stronger the higher we climbed. Eventually, we reached a very tiny church on the highest prominence. The religious reprieve was an Orthodox Russian church constructed by previous Russian researchers that had been stationed on King George Island.

The miniature vestibule at the entrance provided a short break from the harsh outdoors. My eyes were drawn to all the gold-plated portraits of Christ and relics that peppered the room. An area for lighted candles adorned the entrance. Dave lit a candle as I took four steps forward to explore the entirety of the rest of the tiny church's interior. It's amazing that people would make the mammoth effort to construct a church in such a remote location, building under some of the most difficult conditions imaginable. The importance of religion to some knows no boundaries drawn on a map and is sensitive to no weather. I've always found religion a difficult concept to handle in my personal life. In my logic, there are countless varying religious and belief systems around the world based in different cultures. What is the probability that the one that works best for you, and puts your soul and mind in the best place, is the one you were born into? Traveling, and therefore being exposed to and learning about the many alternatives to Christianity (for me), has been the best way to dabble in new beliefs. Taking small pieces from multiple thought processes allows me to create a patchwork system that works for me. Dysfunctional? Yes. Am I content with it? Absolutely not, but that's why I'll keep searching.

Working in emergency medicine muddles everything. Like any other nurse, paramedic, doctor, firefighter, or police officer, I have witnessed "miracles" for lack of a better word, really something that cannot be explained by science or normal logic. I observe people survive massive traumas, cardiac arrests, and so forth that within any reasoning should not still be living. On days like these it is impossible not to find myself thinking, *Okay, maybe someone upstairs gave us some help on that one.*

Yet in the same day, you can see a mother diagnosed with cancer, a child die, and horrific cases of abuse and neglect that cause you to wonder, *How could a higher power let something like this happen in the world?*

My work has greatly confused my beliefs, but that is why I feel the need to create my own system to achieve happiness. Even so, I lit a candle and said a short prayer for lost loved ones, and for my Kiwi buddy Kevin who was taken too soon. As I placed the candle back in its wooden holder, I watched the light flicker over the black letter K printed on the toe of my left shoe.

Nico looked up and smiled at both of us as we exited the warmth of the miniature Russian chapel to the unwelcome icy breeze. He led us over to the edge of a steep embankment, and the grin on his face slowly widened. Gazing outward from here, the entire second half of the run course was visible, a small path snaking its way through the snowbanks and back out to the sea. Looking down the slope, it appeared that little gullies had formed in the snow leading back down towards the research base. It became evident that those little gullies had been created by the backsides of daring Navy men sliding down the steep slope. He gestured with his hand towards the edge, a big grin on his face, and said, "Vamos!"

Nico disappeared first with a loud, "Wahoo!" Dave followed suit quickly behind him. For just one more second, I took in the beautiful, untainted view of frozen paradise, and then I jumped.

Sliding down, the friction caused the snow to shoot up and under my jacket, coating my back in a layer of skin-tingling snow. It was barely noticeable, softened by the absolute rush of the moment. These are the experiences I craved. The out-of-the-norm snippets of joyous life that happen by random circumstance and which could just as likely never have happened if a particular set of events didn't precede them. Every single minute of my time on this remote continent was special and irreplaceable—not a second was taken for granted.

It seemed like no time had gone by and I was on a plane back to Chile, and just a few days after that, a different plane back to America. Just as when I had returned from Australia, I reflected upon how this unique experience had changed me, and more specifically what it had done for my mind.

These remote races had already begun to restore my passion for running. After running through the mountains of Australia and now the incredible frozen continent of Antarctica, I could truly appreciate the newly found importance of trail running to me. What had started out of necessity to escape the oppression now represented by cities, had flourished in to a love far beyond a simple alternative to urban running. Seeing the beautiful, remote places of the world on my own two feet had been the most therapeutic relief I'd felt. I embraced the purity of the isolation, cherishing the primitive instinct to run for the sake of running itself, not for anyone or anything else.

As on my last two trips, it was the people that shaped my experi-ence as much as the place itself. Fellow runners that I had known for less than a week became closer and dearer to me than people I had known for over a decade. A commonality existed amongst us and I've come to find that people who choose to run 26.2 miles in these wild places around the world have a very easy time getting along and make fast friends. They aren't afraid to share their true stories, their thoughts, problems, or demons, creating an environment that is open, honest, and genuine. It's a community that I felt I belonged in, one where I felt comfortable explaining my true reason for running the continents. This was some-thing that I did not share with many people for a very long time, some not even until now. Although in my own mind this mission was quite clearly aligned with my efforts to recover emotionally and mentally from the marathon bombing, to many around me it remained just a random series of adventures. For the most part I let it stay that way, preferring to keep my ongoing trauma separate from my daily life and relationships.

Yet, somehow I found speaking about the marathon bombing to these fellow runners wasn't as difficult as talking to others. Without saying a word, I knew they understood in some way or another as a runner my pain, the hurt, and the conflict in the feelings that now sur-rounded my sport. The relief that that understanding gave me paralleled the therapy of running the race itself. These are people I would stay in touch with frequently, going on to visit their own countries, and plan trips around the world with.

The more I thought about this epic adventure as a whole, the more I finally felt that I was beginning to close the chapter of my life tainted by the Boston Marathon bombing. A combination of the travel itself and the consequent reward of the amazing people you meet along the way were enough to make me realize that the world is mostly a good place. This belief, stolen from me by the events of 2013, once again took root, slowly blooming to spill out on to the rest of my life. For the next few months, I was finding it easier to travel through cities, loud noises bothered me less, and I was able to not panic if I ever noticed a backpack unattended. Certain traits and habits acquired from being victimized by a terror attack will always remain, but I felt in control of my life again. Emotionally, I was feeling more stable and at peace, to the point where nightmares hardly ever plagued me.

I started to come to terms with the fact that although I couldn't see it at the time, maybe the marathon bombing was a blessing in my life. Had it never happened, it's unlikely I would have ever escaped from my comfort zone to see what a beautiful place the world really is.

Staying true to my passion for the *because I said I would* movement, I could not just call it quits here, even though I believed I had achieved what I first set out to accomplish in healing myself. I made a commitment to run a marathon on every continent, and after graduating from college the following spring, all I had to do was choose the next adventure. It was a pretty good situation to be in and for the first time in awhile, I was content with my life.

CHAPTER SIX

A NEW KIND OF PAIN

Beesands, England
February 2017

I knew something was wrong the moment I looked at my phone. I returned from my run to see an endless stream of messages, notifications, and missed calls on my lock screen. My heart sank. After a run, I have the bad habit of gluing my eyes to my cell phone for the first few minutes before I attend to anything else. This time, as I scrolled through the notifications, I did not feel popular, I felt scared. Sometimes the presence of an inexplicable dread in your heart tells you something isn't right well before you have the logic to explain why.

Most of the messages and voicemails were from coworkers at the hospital or friends that I spent a lot of time hiking with. With my ear pressed tightly to the phone, I listened to the recorded messages from my colleagues. Their voices were played back to me in thready, shaking tones, asking me to call them as soon as I could.

It was late in the day on December 8th when I finally worked up the courage to call Shaina Haley, one of my closest friends at work and a regular hiking partner. A lump formed in my throat as the ringing of the call echoed through the speaker. Sweat rolled down the back of my neck and it felt like an eternity before Shaina's voice replaced the worrisome ringing.

As soon as I heard her speak, the voice coming through in a tone unfamiliar to me, a fresh wave of hollow dread hit me in the chest and I braced myself for what was to come. I do not remember the exact dialogue which Shaina used to tell me, the memory of that initial moment is too painful to be relived or remembered. While choking back tears, Shaina informed me that Rachel, had died.

My body and mind were suddenly suspended in a state of numbness. As the news Shaina had just delivered began to process, coldness crept over my entire body and disbelief churned through me. Hundreds of questions whirred through my brain. Just the day before I had worked a shift with Rachel. The details were muddled at first, but all Shaina could tell me for certain was that Rachel had taken her own life.

I will forever remember that last shift, Rachel seemingly as happy as you can be dealing with all of the drama and BS that an emergency room brings. She was always the one to make us laugh, conjuring smiles throughout the busyness of a workday with her casual banter and cheesy jokes. I remember talking to her about cider donuts and a hike up Mount Isolation in the near future. When we weren't actually working, almost every conversation we had revolved around the White Mountains of New Hampshire. Despite Rachel's normally playful demeanor, when she spoke about the mountains that she loved so much, there was a poetic beauty to her words. Rachel had recently completed the New Hampshire forty-eight, an impressive feat attempted by many hikers in the Northeast. This entails reaching the summit of the forty-eight mountains in New Hampshire that are higher than 4,000 feet, showcasing some of the best scenery the state has to offer. She was a wealth of knowledge and made every hike a comedic experience with her witty humor. She was a regular person who was easy to relate to, but her kindness and consideration far surpassed normal.

In the hospital, Rachel would often be seen comforting patients and families more than any nurse would be expected to do in the time constraints of their shift. The true compassion in her heart easily transcended the bounds of the job description of an emergency room nurse.

A few days later Shaina, our friend Dave, Dave's wife, and I drove to Rachel's home state of Pennsylvania to attend her services. We spent the nine-hour drive reminiscing, telling stories, and stopping at breweries to lighten the mood. But the somber undertone remained, anticipation of the unavoidable sadness that would come the next day when seeing her husband and the rest of her family. I was just glad to be in this together with my friends; I wasn't equipped to see the anguish of her family alone.

At the funeral home, we were graciously welcomed with much appreciation for having driven from New Hampshire. In the background as people mingled and recalled stories, I noticed a slideshow playing on a TV, compiled from photos over the years and artistically put together by my friend and true outdoor mentor, Jim Gagne. The photos came from all parts of Rachel's life, some from her mother, some from us, and many from even before we had met her. Regardless of the context, each photo showed Rachel wearing a vibrant smile, one that radiated through the screen, and which made me wonder how she was able to conceal so much pain. There was no surprise that almost every single picture from recent years was of her on a mountain. We smiled at each memory, and then cried as each photo passed realizing that we had all had our last hike with Rach.

As the pictures continued to scroll somberly on the screen, like a funeral procession in its own right, my heart skipped a beat when a photo of us together popped up. The pressure in my chest released and I wept hard, but silently. I mourned for her, my friends, her family, and her husband.

After learning that Rach had taken her own life, I was left with so many questions. Someone I thought I knew so much about and had even worked with hours before it happened—how did I not see anything coming? I struggled with this question every day from the moment I first heard the news of her tragic and untimely death. I thought about Rach and the hikes we had done and the hikes she promised to do with me in the future, which were now nothing but a memory of empty words.

Hiking is sacred because I believe it brings out purity and goodness in people that would otherwise remain hidden by the strains of everyday life. When spending time in the woods, all the stress contrived from modern existence disappears and suddenly you're able to clearly focus on what you need to. It's therapeutic in the most primitive sense. For this reason, my hiking friends are generally who I consider to be my closest because we tend to understand each other a bit better.

Rachel and I had spent hours upon hours in the woods together, discussing anything and everything imaginable. She knew all about my life, my relationships, my flaws, and my ambitions. I thought I knew hers as well, but in the time following her death, I questioned whether I really knew her at all. Suicide cruelly steals your memories of a person, twisting them with doubt and uncertainty.

When something like that happens to a friend, you revisit every moment together; every hike, every day of work, straining each neuron in your brain to remember the minute details of every conversation you ever had—searching for something, for anything. Even as I write this now, just over a year later, my mind still burns with the question I will never get an answer to, and the one that hurts every time I think of her. Why? What would cause her to go to such extremes when there was seemingly so much love and beauty in her life? She had a wonderful husband, a large group of friends, a successful career, and the White Mountains on her doorstep where she spent the majority of her free time.

That winter was just as snowy as any other in New England but it felt much more cold and considerably more lonely than usual. With these events still painfully fresh, I returned to planning the next adventure, for which I'd be departing the following month in late January. The time spent between finishing the most recent continent race in Antarctica and that next winter was tumultuous and life-changing on many fronts, but not all necessarily in a bad way.

Now that I had graduated from college and was a proper "adult," I still refused to conform to the rigid life plan set out by societal expectations. I moved out of school and began to work an incredible amount of hours to fund my future travels. Additionally, it was illogical for me to commit to an apartment lease when I knew over the next couple of years I would be leaving the country for months at a time. Fortunately, I had some good friends that were willing to offer out couch spaces and air mattresses; I stayed with my parents when I could, and would otherwise sleep nestled in the back of my Toyota RAV4 between my road bike, skis, and surfboard.

Up until the time of Rachel's death, I was busy beyond belief between work and training for whatever the next event might be. Travel remained notably and painfully absent in my life, aside from a quick journey to Chicago to run the marathon and catch up with the couple I had met in Nicaragua, Robby and Mickey. What I realized, especially after the emotional trauma of losing Rachel, is that I needed to keep traveling and exploring to maintain a healthy balance in my life. December was a difficult month for my mental health and the plane ticket I had booked to Paris at the end of January was all but holding me together.

Australia and Antarctica had taught me that the races I truly desired were remote and wild. For that reason alone, I decided that Africa was about as wild as I could get, but in my research I found that flying through Europe was as cheap if not cheaper than flying directly to Africa. Additionally, I discovered a stunningly beautiful race along the cliffs of the southern coast of the U.K. The promo video showed a stark landscape with waves crashing angrily against the rock, accompanied by thrilling and adventurous music had me ready to sign up as soon as I could figure out the conversion from U.S. dollars to pound sterling. Before heading to Africa, Europe would serendipitously end up being continent number four.

On one of the few days where I was not working or running, I laid out a spreadsheet on my computer while sipping coffee in a small café in New Hampshire. Typing furiously into my laptop, I searched dozens and dozens of flights. The new budget airlines from Iceland made it cheaper to get from the east coast of the U.S. to Europe now than it would be to fly west to California. It was a simple project really that just required a bunch of legwork, all I would have to do is find the cheapest city to fly to in Europe from Boston. Once in Europe, travel is so inexpensive that I would then find the cheapest city to fly to Africa from and figure out how to get there as I went. While getting from my entry to departure city in Europe, I would have a little Euro-trip and visit old friends that I had met elsewhere in the world over the past couple of years. In my mind, the plan was genius and a great excuse to just get away again.

The Christmas season ended as quickly as it started, though the holiday joy never really set in, persistently overshadowed by my grief for Rachel. Work was a reminder, the mountains were a reminder, and, as had become a common theme in my life, running just gave me too much time to think. As it had done in the past, the thought of upcoming travel ignited hope—hope at the prospect of healing through the freedom and adventure awaiting me in far off lands.

Still not being keen on spending time in large cities, I departed Paris less than forty-eight hours after I arrived. My primary purpose of being in the U.K. was this marathon on the remote coast; an urban jungle in France was just taxing on my mental state. At least flying to London, I had the hope in my heart that the English hills would provide the isolated beauty that I sought.

Even though tall buildings still encased me everywhere I looked, walking around London, I was flooded by a feeling of absolute childish giddiness. Strolling up and down old cobblestone streets and darting into narrow alleyways between ancient-looking homes, this city was surprisingly enjoyable. I lived up to my American tourist stereotype and was enthralled by the fact that everything reminded me of Harry Potter or Sherlock Holmes. Each time I saw a double-decker bus or one of the unmistakable red telephone booths, I would feel as though I was striding through the scene of a movie. Adding to the excitement of venturing to London, my buddy Dave Cooper, an Aussie who I had met diving in Honduras, graciously offered to host me in his and his wife Kate's flat. Having only ever known Dave wearing board shorts, it was quite the change to see him bundled up in the cold London air. Being able to catch up with him and meet Kate was undoubtedly the highlight of my brief time in London. Exiting the city however, my bubbly mood faded as I realized how foolish I had been in planning to get to the start line of the upcoming marathon.

Almost as if I was seventeen again, signing up for the Philadelphia Marathon without thinking of the logistics of arriving there, I was now again in the same predicament. My race the upcoming weekend was apparently in a rather tricky spot to get to. Attempting to be proactive, I connected with a woman on the CouchSurfing website who offered to host me at her home, which was close to the race, but unfortunately she could not drive me all the way to the start. Additionally, the rural British countryside had very limited options for public transit to specific towns, and Uber was certainly nonexistent. Turning to the Facebook page for the race, I typed my plea for a ride and sent it out to the running world in which I had always found the best examples of camaraderie. Sure enough, my fleet-footed friends answered my prayers when a woman named Elizabeth agreed to pick me up on her way to the race. Funny thing though, I never told Elizabeth exactly where I would be staying with my CouchSurfing host. As Elizabeth and I plotted logistics, now just days before the race, we realized a crucial error: where I would be staying was way off the beaten path, too far for her to retrieve me. Thus, it was with an incredible amount of trust and kindness she offered to host me the night before the race and bring me to the start line the next morning. She then sent me an explicit set of instructions for my journey, involving a train to Exeter and a particular bus to the town of Chudleigh where she would meet me with her car.

The weather I experienced during my travel day to meet her was everything you would expect from the coast of the United Kingdom in wintertime: rainy, cold, and windy enough to overpower an umbrella. When I arrived in Exeter, my spirits fell when I learned that it would be about three more hours until I could hop on the bus I needed.

Now slogging down the brick-laid streets of Exeter, my pack grew more and more wet, soaking through until I could feel its sticky dampness on my back. This was one of the difficulties about traveling through so many different seasons in one trip. Not only did I have cold winter-wear for Europe, but also hiking equipment for Africa, warm weather clothes, and diving equipment all piled atop each other. Now this mass of gear and clothes were saturated, weighing me down as I splashed through the increasing amounts of puddles on the sidewalk.

Drenched and chilled to the bone, I stumbled through the doors of a corner pub and took a booth to myself. My wet pants squeaked in protest against the worn leather booth as I sat down. Over the course of the next hour, I wolfed down the best plate of fish and chips I had ever had, in the nation where it was born. The perfectly battered fish served under crisp newspaper with a pint of smooth ale dramatically lifted my spirits. With a belly full of fish and beer, I happily trotted towards the bus station, through streets now strewn with newly created rivers.

When Elizabeth picked me up after the sleepy, dark bus ride, we exchanged brief greetings before she showed me to a warm shower in her and her husband's home. I optimistically hung my wet clothes to dry before morning, as I would not be returning here after the race. Anything warm would have felt magical to me at this point, but a shower was pure heaven. Not wanting to be rude to my host, I made it a quick one, cringing as the cold air replaced the warm water on my skin once I turned the shower off. I dried myself quickly with a borrowed towel and returned down the carpeted stairs that squeaked a tune with each step.

Digging through my pack, I sat quietly in their living room and prepared my race kit for the next day. Being a trail race and slightly longer than a marathon, my prep was more than a normal road race; I had finally learned my lesson regarding the differences between the two very different types of events. In the kitchen, Elizabeth and her husband were busy cooking a large meal that smelled insanely delicious to my empty stomach and gluttonous nose. Fighting my senses and trying to impose as little as possible, I ate a Clif Bar from my bag, and finished organizing my kit before announcing I was heading up to bed. We had an early morning, needing to be up at five a.m. to make the nearly hour-long drive down to the teeny tiny coastal town of Beesands.

"Off to bed already?!" Elizabeth asked with a surprised look on her face. She placed another plate down on the dinner table as she said so.

"Well, I thought I'd let you two eat and get ready for the morning!" I felt kind of silly now for retiring so early in the night.

"Bobby, don't be ridiculous! The food is for all of us, come down and eat!" She smiled and gestured towards a chair.

Walking myself back down the stairs, I joined the two of them in my first home-cooked meal since leaving the United States. It was just as delicious as it had smelled earlier, even bettering the mood-changing fish and chips from earlier that day. Once again, my belly full, I went upstairs, set my alarm, and drifted off to sleep, ready to run through the green English countryside as soon as the sun rose.

Every race morning comes differently to me and there still appears to be no rhyme or reason to how I'll feel before an event. Even as a more experienced marathon runner now, I still often feel incredibly anxious before some races and not at all for others with seemingly no pattern to it. The only consistency I found was the feeling of the need to vomit before (and after) every college cross-country race.

This morning I woke up to an impeccable calm in Elizabeth's chilly guest room. Better than that, there was now an absence of the pitter-patter of raindrops on the roof, which had become the soundtrack of my night.

Trail races had started to make running exciting again because I could never anticipate what would happen over the strenuous and varied course of 26.2-plus miles. Road running had mostly lost its appeal to me; it felt like a predictable story, the same thing every single time. But when I prepared for a race like today, it gave me this childish illusion of suiting up for battle. I placed every single item carefully and methodically into my running pack, I had this down to a science now—first aid supplies, headlamp, extra layers, survival blanket, ample amount of candy bars, et cetera. Everything I needed to get through the next who-knows-how-many hours was set to go. This was yet another thing that excited me about trail running, you never truly knew how long your adventure would last. The course elevation and the elements can change so much that the distance is far from the only variable needed to calculate a time. If there potentially was a pattern emerging in the calm versus anxiety prerace feelings, it seemed to support my theory that I belonged on the trails.

Elizabeth's car swerved tightly around the corners of the excessively tall hedges that lined the dark country roads like a stunt driver on a movie set. Headlights were our only guidance to light the way while the sun still lingered beyond the horizon.

Finally arriving to the parking area, I could hear the *squish* of the mud under the tires when we pulled onto the grass. Having rained the previous few days, I already knew it was going to be extremely muddy and wet out there. The *squish* was even louder under my shoes when I swung my legs out of the car and onto the soaking ground. A grin grew across my face; today was going to be a blast.

Elizabeth was running the ultra-distance, so her race began earlier than mine. We checked in and I eavesdropped on her race briefing to learn more about the terrain we would be dealing with. Over the fifteen-minute speech by the race director, the one thing that I gathered was that it wouldn't be easy. I wished Elizabeth luck and headed back into the registration tent to try and keep warm until my race began.

They announced the briefing for my distance was beginning so I made my way over to the crowded group of runners. Once again, the race director welcomed the new group to the Endurance Challenge Series South Devon event.

"Who's traveled the furthest to be here today?" he shouted loudly over the buzz of chattering runners. A few town names were chirped out, tinged with proper British accents, and then I piped up.

"Boston, Massachusetts!" I yelled out.

Every single person in the tent turned to stare at me.

"Wow, you must be joking mate! How in the Christ did you find yourself down here? No bother, we're happy to have ya, yank!" The crowd murmured and laughed and he carried on with the safety briefing.

What he continued to emphasize the most was how the heavy rainfall had intensified the mud all over the course making some of the steep downhill sections abnormally tricky.

"Although you must be mindful of your footing, please do try and keep your head up. It's a beaut' of a course and you won't want to miss it, lads." He paused one more time then abruptly stated, "We start in five, enjoy it!"

No matter what I'm feeling the morning before a race, in those last few minutes before the gun, there is always a surge of excitement that pulses through my veins. As I stood shaking my legs out on the starting line, adrenaline flowed freely through my vessels, hyping me up and preparing my body for the next few hours of intensity.

The gun sounded and many took off sprinting up the steep and slippery grassy hill that started the race. Myself and the many others who had learned this lesson the hard way let them run past while we hung back and slowly grinded up the unrelenting grass ascent. Upon cresting the first of many tests that day, the sparkling Atlantic Ocean came into view, strong and roaring.

Gazing ahead, the single-track trail could be traced through the grassy fields, following a path that twisted high above the ocean atop amazing stark cliffs for miles and miles. Somewhat shockingly for a coastal U.K. day in winter, the sun began to shine down, shimmering off the turbulent water. It amazed me how loud the crashing waves sounded even so far below me, striking the barren cliffs with such force that it was impossible not to be reminded of the respect the ocean deserves.

Once again, as was becoming habitual over the past few years, I lifted my head towards the sky and thanked the universe for placing me here. If it were not for this race, there is no way I would ever have ventured to the tiny coastal town of Beesands in such a remote piece of the U.K. Yet because of my journey and the mission I had set for my healing mind, this is where I ended up, and I could not have been more thankful. Running along the stunning cliffs, the ocean crashed upon my left side and endless rolling fields of green protected me on the right, the contrast between the wildness of one and the peace of the other making each all the more alluring. A maze-like network of hedges and patchwork designs like you would see from an airplane highlighted the beauty of the far-from-ordinary grasslands.

More than half the race had gone by when the course finally departed from the coastal trail and turned inland towards the expansive meadows. Right away the battle with the mud began. It was literally everywhere. At first it was just as fun as I expected it to be. There's just something about getting your clothes and shoes dirty that make you feel like you're really working hard. However, the incredible amount of mud was relentless and began to seep and cake inside my trail shoes. At mile eighteen it was annoying and by mile twenty-three it was downright uncomfortable, pressing irritatingly on points of my toes normally sheltered from the abuse of the trail.

For miles I had been on my own, and now the discomfort with my feet was becoming more and more mentally cumbersome. A loud, "Oy!" startled me and I turned to see a wide-shouldered runner in a bright yellow top approaching from behind.

"You're that bloke from Boston, aren't ya?" he asked, catching his breath between words.

I laughed. "Yep, that's me!"

"You didn't come all the way down here just for the race did you? Because that would be bloody stupid! We're in the middle of nowhere!" He chuckled and wiped the sweat from his brow.

"Actually, I kinda did," I could feel my face turning red, "but you can't beat these views."

"I hear ya on that one brother. Well, welcome to our humble corner of the world. Enjoy the run, mate."

We pressed on together for a while before I eventually picked up the pace on the next section of flat, taking me through the old wooden gates of a sheep pasture. Dodging placid white balls of fluff, my pace quickened, spurred by that always fulfilling sensation that the end of the race was near.

Finally, over the next hill, I saw the finish line billowing in the wind, far below me in the valley. Rain started to sprinkle and the gusts started to pick up just as I made my way across the line to the light applause of no more than twenty people, all donning waterproof jackets.

A stout rosy-cheeked woman strung the yellow-ribboned medal around my neck and wished me a hearty "congratulations" in a smooth British accent. Elizabeth and her husband ran over almost immediately to ask about what I thought of the race.

"Way harder than I thought, but so amazingly beautiful! I had no idea that England could look like this!" I waved my hand around gesturing to the surrounding landscape. "How'd you do? You finished quick!"

She grinned broadly and then her husband was the one to say it: "She won! First woman and fifth overall!" He beamed with pride.

"Wow! Well done! That's amazing!" I held up my hand for a high-five. Elizabeth clapped her hand around mine and we walked over to wait for her to be awarded her prize.

After the ceremony, Elizabeth graciously agreed to drive me to the closest train station in the town of Totnes where I would ride back to London. They told me not to worry as I dragged an unholy amount of mud into the backseat of their vehicle. Rain continued to splatter across the windshield of the car the entire ride to the train station. An unforgettable smell of soaked polyester and sweat circulated through the vehicle that was only strengthened by the heat.

In less than a half hour, I found myself saying goodbye and giving two smelly hugs to my new friends. All they had done for me was remarkable, especially after having never met before and with such minimal interaction prior to my arrival. It was another one of the countless examples of kindness and camaraderie that I have experienced within the trail-running community.

Thankfully they were able to drop me off at the community center in Totnes where I'd be able to pay to take a shower and clean myself up before my train was scheduled to leave. I walked through the doors of the center covered in dirt, my long brown hair matted and tangled, mud and rain coating my beard, and my large travel pack straining against my shoulders. A short elderly woman with horn-rimmed glasses at the reception desk peered over her glasses at me as soon as I stepped inside.

"Can I help you, sir?" she asked skeptically, a tinge of worry in her voice.

I quickly realized by her tone that I was probably a sight for sore eyes. "Um, yes. Is it possible to take a shower here?"

The woman looked somewhat relieved by my response. "Yes, of course. It will cost two pounds."

I handed her the coins from my pocket and rejoiced in the fact that that was most likely the best money spent today. She directed me to the gentlemen's locker room around the back of the hall, adorned with an endless array of colorful posters advertising different exercise programs. At the end of the corridor, I pushed the wooden door to the shower room open and stained the tile floor with my muddy shoes.

First, I put down my bag against the lockers in the far corner of the room; I wanted to keep it as clean as possible from all the dirt covering my body that was sure to go flying as I stripped down. Thankfully I was the only person in the quiet locker room because removing the wet clothes that now stuck to my skin like suction cups ended up being quite the process. It would have been impossible to recognize the deep blue color of my Salomons when I removed them from my feet, every inch of them caked in thick mud. The socks underneath were almost black and wreaked a terrible odor when they were finally exposed to the air. Peeling them off I noticed the white, swollen, and blistered skin underneath, the surface pruned from the hours of soaking. Mud and sweat impregnated my running tights that had all but adhered to my skin. With a bit of odd maneuvering and lots of pulling, they slid off with a lively *pop*. Now naked, I made my way over to the showers, the smooth tile pressed cold against my defeated feet. All alone in the communal shower, I pressed the shiny silver button against the wall for water. It steamed and poured from the nozzle for five or six seconds then stopped suddenly. I pressed it again and the same thing happened...and again, and again. In what had to be the most annoying design in the world, if you would like a continuous flow of water the button would have to be held constantly. Eventually I figured out that I could stand backwards and keep my butt pressed up against the button to get round this aggravating plumbing obstacle. The whole ordeal was a huge pain in the ass.

Clean as possible, I made my way back to the lockers, dried myself off, and put on warm, dry clothes that felt otherworldly. Gathering my soggy mud-tinged race garments into a giant ball of muck; I placed them into a garbage bag to wash them at the next city I would pass through. The only item left on the agenda was to clean my shoes as best as possible so they would not streak mud all over the inside of my comparatively clean pack.

The white gleam of the sink caught my eyes. I felt bad about doing it, but truly went above and beyond to clean as thoroughly as possible afterwards. When I turned to place the last shoe back on the ground, I accidentally activated the motion sensor on the hand dryer. *Perfect!* I thought. So I spent the next fifteen minutes drying my shoes under the subtle blast of the lukewarm dryer. This was traveling. This was an unconventional life on the road—and I loved it.

Feeling like a new man, I stopped by the local pub for a well-deserved pint, and two hours later was on a train back to London. Although I felt dry and clean, my muscles still ached with the pains of the day and I was not entirely thrilled to be sleeping on a bench in the train station that night. Because of flight schedules and budgeting, it didn't make sense for me to book a place to stay in London. Instead, I would rest as comfortably as possible and then at four a.m. take a bus to Heathrow Airport to catch a plane to Oslo, Norway.

Without any further plans for the night I strapped my pack around my legs, moved my passport and wallet to my inside chest pocket, and drifted off to sleep in the midst of the hustle and bustle of Paddington Station.

The night in Paddington went by quicker than I anticipated and I was only awoken once by a garbage man checking to make sure I was alive. The short flight to Norway was just as uneventful and allowed even more sleep for my tired body.

In Oslo, I visited Hanne, the girl I had met on a sunny beach in remote Nicaragua two years prior. She was graciously able to take a break from her studies to travel through Spain with me for a week, a welcome change to the cold and dark Norwegian winter.

Although our trip created lasting memories, my head was in a different place, and my heart wasn't in the experience. Though physically present, my mind constantly wandered to thoughts of Rachel. It had now been two months since her death and the "why?" question occupied every second of free thought my brain would allow.

When Hanne and I hiked in the beautiful mountains of Montserrat, my first real hike since Rachel died, I found myself frequently looking to the sky and asking for answers. In an extremely religious region of Spain, I thought just maybe the big guy upstairs could do me a favor and give me a sign. I would have taken anything he could throw at me that would give some sort of inkling as to why Rachel had left this earth so soon. This beautiful, beautiful planet that was full of the things she loved. This wasn't like the Boston Marathon bombing that had changed the chemistry of my thoughts and reactions so resolutely and extremely, incapacitating me to the point of anguish. More so, my pain from Rachel's death was an unwanted visitor, encroaching frequently and residing in the everyday reminders that would pop into my head. Most consistently, I could always count on the lonely despair recurring anytime I set foot on a mountain. Even from an ocean away I associated the rocky trails and scenic vistas with the countless memories Rachel and I had created back home in New Hampshire. What would make her hurt so badly that she would not want to see the beauty of a mountaintop ever again?

This constant distraction made my time with Hanne seem like it had never really happened at all. And before I knew it, I was on a plane to Portugal while she was headed back to the chilly Norwegian winter. For someone who advocates so much for living in the present moment, I sure as hell was doing a terrible job at it these past few weeks.

My European trip continued thanks to a brief and very minimally investigated internet search which revealed a website called Surf Nomads, offering unique surf lessons with locals in various locations around the globe. I was put in touch with a man named Russo who agreed to host me for just over a week and bring my rudimentary surfing to a more advanced level. After two connecting flights and a long train ride, he picked me up in his pickup at the station in Aljezur. By no means was this the easiest place to get to, but my God was it beautiful.

Every day, Russo and his buddy Nelson would kick my ass in the lineup to the point where my body felt like it had undergone a marathon in the ocean. The water was cold and the waves were strong, pummeling me again and again on day one. I could barely feel my feet and my lungs cried from the abuse and oxygen deprivation. Each time I wanted to paddle in and end my session it was always just, "one more wave." I knew how to surf, but I came to this small spot in Portugal so they could teach me how to surf well. In credit to both of them, they were very committed to making sure that I held up my end of the deal by giving one hundred percent each and every day.

Battered and bruised after the first day, I wasn't sure I wanted to keep going at this pace, even shredding the left leg of a wetsuit in the first few hours. The combination of Rachel weighing heavily on my mind and being obliterated by the ocean meant I was feeling defeated beyond belief. Russell and Neil were relentless in the best way possible; they did not let me quit and they pushed me to be more comfortable in the ocean than I could have ever imagined. I needed it. Each day I would fall asleep before my head hit the pillow with muscles I didn't even know existed crying out for mercy.

Every session brought new challenges and tested both my physical and mental strength in ways running had not touched upon before. Persistence paid off and soon I was catching waves I could have never dreamed of, my intense focus upon the ocean pushing worrying thoughts far out of my mind. My time spent with these two gents was the perfect medicine of distraction. After surfing we would often fish (I later found out illegally) for our dinner and I would listen to stories of big wave competitions and improbable legends and tales from their youth. I knew each morning when I woke up that every ounce of daylight was to be filled with straining physicality in the pursuit of adventure and perfect waves.

Driving to and from surf spots on rough and windy dirt roads, I started to notice the unassuming beauty in this small corner of Portugal. We were far enough from any city that the only semblance of modernism was the wind turbines in the distance, which evoked a splendor of their own. The lush green vegetation contrasting with the deep brown cliffs and beige sand dunes held magnificence beyond words. Uninterrupted days of clear blue skies allowed the sunshine to illuminate it all, signaling to me that no matter how exhausted I was from surfing, I needed to run here.

The following days brought yet more grueling sessions with Russo and Nelson that left every muscle burning, but with a marathon in Africa now only two weeks away, I really did need to put some legwork in. Russo had told me there were loads of "kind of" cleared trails behind his property that I could keep myself busy on for as long as I'd like. Checking my watch one evening, I knew I had a couple of hours until dark, so I swapped out my wet suit for running shorts and set out.

Running down the hill behind the house, I ended up engulfed in the thickly clustered trees in no time. Heavy brush covered the soft dirt path that quickly transitioned into red clay that felt heavenly under my shoes. Each stride felt better than the last as my foot strikes were cushioned by the soft clay earth, a sensation surely like that of running on clouds. Thick beads of sweat covered my face when I began to push up a steep hill out of the valley that I had so easily descended into. With no map to orient me, the only sense of direction guiding me was the sound of crashing waves in the distance. Tortured from the repetitive beatings of those same waves, my legs screamed as I ran faster and faster up the hill. I could see the top now, one final push, and I yelled as I crested over the hill, then gasped at what I saw.

I now stood on the edge of a cliff, staring out into a bright sea of blue ocean with the sun a vibrant orb of yellow-orange beginning to dip below the horizon. A few puffy white clouds dotted the sky, together forming the shape of a crescent that crowned the majestic evening sun. The salty air tickled my nostrils as the waves continuously smashed against the ancient rock walls far, far below. Everything about this moment was perfect. All of my senses felt heightened, and a feeling of urgency to remember each sensation and aspect of this moment overcame me. I sat down and closed my eyes.

Often I reflect on the unique set of feelings travel can arouse. More particularly, the incredibly rare feeling that being where you are right now, in this moment, is exactly where you're supposed to be. This sensation rises through you with a connectedness and energy that is impossible to describe, it can only be experienced. Nothing else matters except clinging to every second and consciously trying to burn every sense of it into your memory, so one day, when you really need it, you can return to it in your mind—listening, hearing, smelling, tasting, and seeing with such intensity that you know you will never forget.

I have only ever experienced this sensation twice; once on the beach, as the sunset over Jiquilillo; and right now, alone on these high cliffs in Portugal. I felt like there was nowhere else I belonged. I was so content with myself in that time and that place, it just seemed like the whole world came together for just that moment.

In that beautiful setting that made everything in the world make sense, I began to cry. Then I yelled louder than I ever had before, knowing I was so far away that no one could hear me. Sobbing for just one more minute, I then looked up to the sky, and began to talk to Rachel.

Our conversation was short and one-sided, but it belonged to us, the Earth, the ocean, and no one else. By no means am I the most spiritual man in the world, but as I sat on that cliff, hearing the sounds of the waves below and feeling the warm wind stream gently over my cheeks, I knew that Rach was listening to me. And it was enough.

Had I known how much this small village in Portugal would have meant to me and how special it was, I would have stayed longer. Unfortunately, now towards the end of my time in Europe, my agenda was tighter and flexibility was not an option any longer. I had to fly to Munich to catch the plane that would bring me to the wild and mysterious continent of Africa for the first time in my life.

The prospect of seeing a corner of the world so new and different to anything I ever had before was thrilling, but the excitement was coupled with a slight feeling of apprehension. The hurt I felt surrounding Rachel's death was very obviously impairing my ability to enjoy the adventure. I struggled to stay present; my preoccupied mind full of thoughts that circled like vultures around my fragile mental state.

I craved closure and an explanation, but unfortunately, in the face of suicide, many questions are left unanswered. I'm sure she was experiencing a pain so dark and so deep she felt that none of us could have understood. But if she would have only said something, or reached out—maybe she did reach out. Did I miss it? These are the thoughts that haunted me, constantly taking me back to reanalyze everything Rachel had said to me in those last few days of her life. Suicide is an action that can never be understood by anyone other than the person who completes the act. I can sympathize with Rach for the pain she must have been feeling, but I will never actually know what it was like for her. For this reason, we cannot fairly judge, blame, or criticize. A person who takes their own life has retreated and been pushed to the darkest corner of human experience, where relief seems no longer a possibility, even if a solution might seem clear to those looking in from the outside. Rationally I knew and understood this to be true. Yet no matter how many times I was told there was nothing I could have done, believing that still felt impossible.

With too much on my mind and too little time to process it, I found myself boarding a train on a frosty morning in Munich on my way to the airport. Regardless of how I felt, I knew that by stepping onto this next plane I was leaving what was familiar to me and about to enter a world far different than any I had known. A wild and new continent with unfamiliar sights, smells and tastes to be had, and full of what I was sure would be unforgettable adventures. Reflecting back on how I ended up here, the Boston Marathon bombing seemed like a lifetime ago. Now, instead of being full of hate and despising that day where my life changed so dramatically, I found I was grateful; grateful that it had led me to this moment where I was boarding a plane to somewhere never previously imagined. So whether my mind was ready or not, I stepped onto a tightly packed plane bound for the central African country of Rwanda.

CHAPTER SEVEN

AN UNEXPECTED ISLAND

Mafia Island, Tanzania
March 2017

Imagine sending $2,000 via wire transfer to some random guy in Tanzania that you had never met before, *but* through a mutual friend you had met last year in Antarctica, you were official Facebook friends. This was the start of my journey to Africa.

My pal Sandy, who I met doing the White Continent Marathon, had told me about the amazing experience he had at the Mt. Kilimanjaro marathon, a race hosted in the outskirts of Moshi, Tanzania near the base of Kilimanjaro. After the marathon, Sandy also hiked the mountain itself, calling it one of the most epic adventures of his life. From that moment on, my mind was pretty well made up which marathon would be the one to take me to the incredible and wild continent of Africa.

Sandy graciously connected me to his guide, Emmanuel, so I could obtain some additional information and begin organizing logistics. Hiking Mt. Kilimanjaro is strictly regulated and requires a guide with all appropriate permits and documentation. As the highest point in Africa, and the least technical of the Seven Summits, it draws up to 25,000 hikers each year. Of that number about forty-five percent summit the isolated volcanic peak in the southeastern corner of the country.

I had messaged Emmanuel the summer after I ran in Antarctica and expressed my interest in running the marathon and trekking Kilimanjaro. After a few weeks of exchanging messages in broken English on Facebook Messenger, I had my trip scheduled for February 2017 with the plan of running the marathon on Sunday, and starting the six-day Kilimanjaro trek early Monday morning. I was told this would only benefit me because my "tired marathon legs" would force me to move at a slower pace, thus improving my acclimatization.

Because of my "connection," the cost of this expedition was not nearly as much as the gargantuan prices I had seen scattered on various travel blogs around the internet. However, my bank account shuddered when I had to front Emmanuel the majority of the money for all the costs involved. Conveniently enough, the only way he could receive payment would be from a bank wire transfer, something I swore I would never do, ever. After fighting every logical voice in my mind saying, No, I drove to the bank to fill out the paperwork necessary for the transfer.

You know it's worrisome when you get to the counter and the bank teller reviews the paperwork, looks up at you and asks, "Are you sure?"

And the answer was easily a no, but I just had to send it anyway. Emmanuel messaged me the next day confirming he had received the payment and continued to stay in contact with me the following weeks, which certainly settled some of my uneasiness surrounding the sketchy situation.

Right around the time I made this ballsy (stupid) transaction, one of my best friends from college, Ryan Sandford, was departing for

Rwanda for his assignment as a Peace Corps volunteer. Considering the fact that Rwanda borders Tanzania, and since not many folks from the Granite State make it over to that corner of Africa, it would be impossible for me to not visit him during my travels. His commitment of twenty-seven months living in an incredibly remote part of a developing country far surpassed any logistical difficulty I might have in adding a few extra flights to my journey.

● ● ●

With my European adventure now behind me, I sat sweating and sticking to the dusty seats in the Addis Ababa Airport on my connection in Ethiopia. For six hours now my flight to Rwanda had been delayed for "technical reasons" with no evidence of a departure on the horizon. Over time I had developed an essential skill involving the ability to sleep in airports under even the strangest of conditions, but this was different. Dirt clung to the roof of my mouth, loud music of a genre I'd never heard before penetrated my eardrums, and it smelled god-awful. I walked countless laps up and down the terminal, passing the prayer rooms, cafes, and many other signs that I couldn't read because of the strange letters that adorned them. No matter how many times I tried, it was impossible to focus on reading the small paperback book I had already been struggling with for the past week.

Additionally, I was also beginning to worry about my excessive tardiness. I had a pretty strict timeline to make it to Ryan's village in a rural part of Rwanda's Southern Province. He had begun sending me voice memos through WhatsApp of important phrases I should know in Kinyarwanda. Like, "amakuru," meaning how are you; "muraho neza," hello; "meze neza," I'm well; "nitwa Bobby," my name is Bobby; and most importantly of all, "simbizi," I don't know.

Ryan needed to teach me some of these phrases in advance because with his hectic teaching schedule in the village, he would be unable to collect me from the airport. Therefore, I needed to take a taxi to a bus station, find the correct bus, and then miraculously get off at a specific point to meet a moto driver named Salomon, who would then take me to the remote village of Kizibere where Ryan lived. This flight delay was now crushing any slim hope I had harbored that everything would run seamlessly, but travel is travel.

After hours of waiting, my plane finally departed safely, and I arrived in the capital city of Kigali, much later than expected. Being totally out of my element, I overpaid for a taxi to the Nyabagogo bus station where I was still the only white person or, "umuzungu" in sight. I was immediately targeted by every single hustler looking to make a quick buck to help me find the correct bus. A short man who knew a few words in English asked where I was going and waved for me to follow him. He brought me to a dusty ticketing counter and requested some Rwandan francs, which equated to about a dollar, and then handed me a ticket, then once again waved for me to follow his quick pace out of the cramped office.

I was on sensory overload. This was everything I had pictured an African city to be, an often imagined scene influenced by Hollywood movies and blended with the realism from better-accredited documentaries: people everywhere, pressing against each other under a burning sun which sat high and alone in a cloudless sky; car horns honking endlessly, mixed in symphony with shouting street vendors, cawing roosters and the call to prayer from a nearby mosque; the smell of burning rubber and rotten fruit assaulted my nares, mingling with the stench of body odor culminating from hundreds of travelers; small children played in the street, barefoot on tough feet, chasing a soccer ball in a game that seemingly never ended.

As I tried to take in everything around me, I realized the man had stopped walking and was pointing to the vehicle in front of us. I handed him a five-dollar bill, his eyes widened and he shook my hand vigorously.

Slowly, I clambered onto a rusty old van that would comfortably seat fifteen people and wedged myself in the middle of eighteen Rwandan locals with my sixty-five-liter pack on my lap. Heat pressed incessantly through the windows and dust clung to the rivers of sweat that ran down the back of my neck.

The best way to describe the erratic yet impressive driving of the short man behind the wheel would be a drunken racecar driver. I say impressive because he managed to avoid hitting the hundreds of people, goats, and chickens that recklessly darted across the dirt streets of Kigali on the way out of town. An unmistakable scent of burning rubbish remained in the air as we wove our way towards the city's peripheries.

After the van incredulously breached the borders of the city unscathed, the ride was pleasant, beautiful even. Suddenly, the trash-ridden corridors were replaced by an endless horizon of farmland and forest. Countryside whirred by the window in streaks of brown, green, and orange. Unable to sleep, or even move at all really, my eyes took in the sight of this beautiful continent for the first time.

As a young child dreaming of adventures, Africa had always found a way to capture my imagination more so than anywhere else. It seemed more exotic, wild, scary, and utterly different than anything in my suburbanite American childhood. Now I was here, in that same land that I had fantasized of exploring, and my florid childhood imagination never would have dreamt up this beginning to my adventure. Sweltering in an overcrowded van, headed somewhere that I could not even locate on Google Maps, praying that a motorbike driver named Salomon would still be waiting for me at a random road crossing hours later than arranged. What you can't conceptualize as a child when you have these spectacular dreams is that this is what adventure truly is—the complete, unglamorous unknown.

Because of the immense language barrier and equal amount of confusion, I missed where I was supposed to get off. Luckily, Salomon was more attentive than the average Uber driver.

I unwittingly got off the bus one stop too far and quickly became the most popular client in Ruhango for a return moto driver. Suddenly, I was swarmed by young men, like bees to a hive, all aiming to cash in big on me. Out of fairness, I chose the first guy to hand me a helmet and we negotiated a price that equated to just under three U.S. dollars. We zipped along through the dark on his moto that made strange rattling noises I tried hard to ignore, up the hills and into the night.

We rounded the corner almost too quickly, momentum from my large pack swayed the bike uncomfortably, and I saw a man frantically waving and jumping up and down in my peripheral vision as we roared passed. I tapped my driver who seemed to be ignoring me; but that was without a doubt, Salomon. This time I gave the inattentive driver a light smack on the side of his helmet causing us to swerve ever so slightly while Salomon pulled up beside us. We shook hands and took off down the dirt roads, big bumps in the pitch dark on a rickety motorcycle. Despite putting all my faith and safety into a moto driver I had never met I still breathed a heavy sigh of relief, knowing I was finally off to see Ryan. Despite what seemed somewhat of an impressive feat, he delivered me there in one piece and dropped me off in front of Ryan's "house."

Ryan's living space was a modest concrete structure deep in the heart of Kizibere and was built by the villagers with the intent to partner with the Peace Corps and receive an American to live in the village for the first time ever. Under the cover of night, I was unable to see much of my surroundings, but I was flooded with happiness when I saw Ryan's face emerge from the doorway. After talking to him about coming to visit for so long, reading his blog posts, and viewing the amazing photos and videos that allowed me to "virtually visit the village" I was actually here.

His lightly bearded face appeared under the light of the moon and he pulled me into a huge hug. He looked healthy, happy, and exactly where he was supposed to be. Truth be told, I can think of no one better than Ryan Sandford to be working alongside the people of Kizibere. His compassion, eagerness to help, and selfless attitude make him the perfect person for this village. Similar to Alex Sheen, every time I ever have a conversation with Ryan it inspires me to become a better person. While we caught up over a couple beers, I began to doze from the exhausting day of travel. I lazily unraveled my sleeping bag with heavy eyelids and quickly fell asleep, bringing an end to my first day in the mysterious and rural land of Rwanda.

The next morning, Ryan had to teach all day. Since I was still exhausted from the borderline stressful journey yesterday, I had no qualms about remaining at Ryan's and hand-washing some of my laundry. Let me tell you, there is no better place to dry clothes than in the equatorial sun of East Africa. Ryan didn't really want me to go out on my own anyway, being slightly concerned about the attention I would garner by surprising the village with an unexpected visitor. Two umozungu there at one time, especially one with a beard and long hair, something incredibly foreign to them, would be a very bizarre and borderline disruptive presence. So I made myself comfortable and read some books while washing my laundry in the small plastic bin behind Ryan's home. All was uneventful until a small child peaked his head around Ryan's wall with a look of shock on his face. "Muraho naza!" I greeted him with a big smile. He came over, shook my hand, and then stood there, staring at me as I picked some flies out of the laundry tub and dowsed my grungy running socks for a fifth time. This went on for about fifteen minutes, him looking me over from head to toe, and me stealing quick glances at him just as shyly. I would look back and smile, give a thumbs-up, and a wave. It was a total and complete language barrier at its finest for me, and major shock value for this young toddler who had no idea what a caveman-looking white dude was doing washing laundry at Lion's home. I say Lion because most of the people in the village call Ryan "Lion," which has nothing to do with any king of the jungle status and is purely a result of the difficulty they had annunciating the R at the beginning of his name.

The boy toddled off just before Ryan came back for lunch. We had the classic Rwandan snack, amandazi, which I would compare to a cubed, stale donut, and sambusa, fried pastry pockets filled with either vegetables or spicy meat—all finished off with some of the freshest fruit I have ever had in my life.

I told Ryan about my encounter and he laughed it off saying I'd be experiencing a whole bunch of that over the next few days. When he first arrived, he experienced similar reactions but said it's no different than just being the new kid in school.

When he went back to teach later that afternoon, more and more kids began to show up around the concrete walls of Ryan's home. Rumor was spreading like wildfire that a second American was in the village, but my formal introduction would have to wait until tomorrow.

We prepared dinner that night with a variety of freshly farmed produce from the village. Meat was a rarity and was often only available when the village decided to kill a goat, which was rather a big deal. And even then, all of it had to be eaten quickly, refrigerators being a luxury notably absent from this rural area. We feasted on banana pancakes, potatoes, a Middle Eastern dish called shakshuka and roasted peanuts, a washing it down with our anti-malarial medication. We ate like kings that night, all under the dim light of a candle flickering atop the small wooden table.

The next morning we awoke at sunrise to run. As the amber glow shone quickly over the wakening farmland, sweat was already dripping from my pale skin. We headed out with one of the Rwandan teachers on a journey through the hills, which would become one of the most special running experiences of my life. The humidity was already nagging at me, smothering us with each stride as we glided up and down the rolling hills. Banana trees blurred by as we sped down the dirt roads, the wind generated by our speed the only relief from the powerful sun. After running a hot and dusty three miles out, we turned around to complete the three miles back in. It was shortly after we had turned around that something quite magical began to happen.

As we were running back into Kizibere, the students of the community school where Ryan taught were also making their way down the dusty road to get to school on time.

Similar to how parents always joke with their children about having to walk to school uphill both ways in a blizzard for miles and miles, these kids actually do that; except instead of a blizzard their obstacle is oppressive heat and humidity.

When they saw us running, some began to join in. They would run for as hard and long as they could and then drop back. As soon as they did, another group of students would be around us, smiling and laughing with uncontrollable joy. The childish innocence and playfulness of that moment makes it one of the best and purest memories I have in my entire life.

This was Ryan's daily life. He had been so integrated and accepted by this community, it was beginning to be a second family. Everything was natural and organic here; it flowed with an indescribable energy. Those who do good are rewarded with a gift far greater than any tangible thing or monetary compensation, a special kind of love and acceptance that transcends all others. This village loved Ryan Sandford and all he was doing to help make it a better place for their children. When I saw all that Ryan had done and is doing, I wasn't surprised. His new name of Lion suited him well in regard to the size of his heart. I could feel the love and passion emanating from him as he spoke about his efforts to leave the village a better place than he found it, because it was now his home.

My time in Ryan's village flew by, teaching me more about joy and community than I had ever learnt on my other travels. Quicker than I would've liked, the week was over. I seamlessly made it back to Kigali with considerably more ease than how I had arrived and was soon on a plane to Tanzania.

• • •

What I envisioned as being one of the most remote, rugged, and wild marathons when I first conceptualized running on seven continents, my choice for Africa actually proved to be the least so in all of those categories. I was so disengaged by the race, I don't even feel like I have much to write about it. Since it lacked all of the previously mentioned adjectives that I had been searching for on this journey, I think the word, "underwhelming" could sum it up nicely. Finishing the race near a crowded stadium in Moshi, I was left disappointed, unfulfilled, and hot.

If it weren't for my first unobstructed view of the profile of Kilimanjaro towering high above the plains, I would venture to say the Kilimanjaro Marathon has nothing to offer except for poor air quality and oppressive heat. The only redeeming quality was the occasional view of the mountain that I would be standing atop of less than a week from now. Its snowcapped peak reflected a vibrant white in the hot African sun, contrasting sharply against a clear blue sky. Wisps of clouds skirted the peak and I imagined what it would feel like to stand atop the highest point in Africa.

There is indeed a benefit to running a marathon the day prior to beginning your ascent of Kilimanjaro. Emmanuel was correct that due to the general fatigue felt from such a race the day before it would cause me to hike slower than my fitness level would normally allow. Therefore, I did myself a favor with the acclimatization to altitude. With that in mind, I also gorged myself on an overabundance of calories to further "help me" in going slow that first day on the mountain.

I finished packing my kit bag with plenty of room to spare and my daypack felt abnormally light, causing me relative concern for the week ahead. This would be the highest altitude I'd ever stood at and I seemingly had less weight in my backpack than what I would carry to a college party. I had packed and meticulously organized each and every piece of gear that Emmanuel said that I would need for the week ahead. Since he had touched the summit of Africa's highest peak over seventy times, I felt good enough about trusting him.

The other reward of running a marathon the day before you start a Kili trek is it goes some way to avoid the jitters of excitement that usually keep you awake the night before a big event. I had not even listened to the full track length of Toto's "Africa" before I was fast asleep under the silky mosquito net covering my bed.

Emmanuel came to collect me from the hotel that he had organized and pulled me into a warm embrace. We had been able to do our pre-hike briefing the previous day, after completing the race, so there was very little to do in preparation aside from getting to the park entrance. To describe to you in its entirety the details of the beginning of my climb up Kilimanjaro would be mundane and redundant in all honesty, but there are a few important components I need to describe before the real action happened.

Very unique to Kilimanjaro, because it is the world's highest freestanding mountain and not part of a larger range, it is made up of five distinct climate zones that change as you ascend the mountain. From bottom to top, a hiker will pass through farmland, rain forest, heather-moorland, alpine desert, and lastly summit climate zones. This also creates a myriad of weather conditions that range from upwards of ninety degrees Fahrenheit in the farmland, to colder than negative ten degrees Fahrenheit at the summit.

The real heroes of Kilimanjaro that face all of these obstacles with unimaginable weight on their backs are the immensely strong porters. A porter could loosely be compared to a Sherpa in the Himalaya. Although not as technically talented and trained in mountaineering as their Nepalese counterparts, in my experience they are just as hardworking and dedicated to their craft. Porters are the backbone of support for hikers attempting Kilimanjaro and do an impossible amount of work for what they are compensated. Under the supervision of the head guide, they are responsible for carrying clients' kit bags, tents, food, and really anything not held in a daypack.

Had I researched a little bit more and found out about the porter system on Kilimanjaro, I would have been slightly less confused as to why Emmanuel told me to leave my sixty-five-liter pack back in Moshi and only bring my sixteen-liter daypack along with the large kit (duffel) bag with me. Stupid me didn't realize I wouldn't be carrying all my own gear and rations. Although this is the norm for Kili, I still felt uncomfortable as a privileged Westerner coming onto this mountain and only having to carry about ten pounds, and then extremely embarrassed once I met the porters who would carry such a colossal amount of gear and equipment.

The porters that would be hiking with us were some of the most interesting and humble people I met while in Tanzania. Although they did not speak much English and Emmanuel had to often play the role of translator, they communicated clearly with facial expressions and enthusiastic emotion—always smiling, always upbeat, laughing, singing, and dancing with an inexhaustible amount of energy. They never wanted me to do more work than I had to and I often fought with them to let me do things on my own. Over the years they are conditioned to be overly helpful and selfless, motivated by the knowledge that those qualities will generate larger tips from affluent foreigners.

Similar to many of the people I encountered in Ryan's village, the porters had very little money, a fact easily exhibited by the dilapidated attire that they hiked in. Many had beaten down flip-flops on their feet, tattered jean shorts, and cotton shirts a few sizes too big. It made my stomach uneasy watching their muscles strain up steep inclines with upwards of sixty pounds on their back while their feet skidded in plastic sandals, all while I watched in my lightweight, moisture-wicking hiking garments. They work tirelessly every single day and are frequently seen grinning from ear to ear, a clear reminder of the lessons I had learned in Central America and most recently, Rwanda. You don't need much to be happy. And those with very little often seem more easily able to be thankful for all they have, not dwelling as much on what they lack; a humbling realization for all of us in the consumerism-driven developed world.

Although I was uncomfortable with the arrangement, I did my best to learn from and share with my new porter friends. Mentally I calculated my finances, trying to increase the tips I could give them upon exiting the park. Daily, I found myself giving away the majority of the chocolate bars I had packed for the trek.

The hiking was beautiful and not particularly challenging for the first few days. The scenery changed regularly as Emmanuel and I passed through the climate zones. Entering the moorland region of the trek, we were no longer in the jungle but rather a place that reminded me of the land of Mordor from *The Lord of the Rings*. Each step was now unsheltered from the tall, tropical tress that previously shielded us from the equatorial suns incessant assault. Although the altitude kept the heat at bay, the strength of the sun was more powerful than anywhere else I had ever been. *Pole, pole,* which translates to "slowly, slowly," is the most common phrase on the mountain and became our mantra as we slowly made our way towards a snow-capped Mount Doom. As we plodded ever closer towards camp, we began to transition into another entirely different set of scenery, this time a lush but rugged landscape full of exotic vegetation, with trees reminiscent of a landscape from a Dr. Seuss book.

The first sign of trouble in my trek came that night when an intense pain in my stomach woke me from my sleep. It felt like someone had reached into my guts and was twisting my intestines around with a barbed probe. Excruciating pangs of pain vibrated through my body and I knew I had to get up and get myself to the latrine. Now at 12,700 feet, the nights were cold, but the brisk air inside my tent was no obstacle given the urgency I now felt.

Wiggling out of my sleeping bag and having to raise my knees to pull socks over my feet provoked the pain even more. Each and every movement felt worse than the last. Finally, I agonizingly unzipped the tent and watched the ice crystals fall in the glow of my headlamp.

Roughly one hundred meters away my salvation, a smelly latrine, stood like a beacon in the distance. I half jogged, half shuffled over for fear of shitting my pants. Suddenly, my head began to pound and spots darted across my field of vision, now I was on my knees on the cold rock. In my haste, I forgot that I needed to travel *pole, pole* at this altitude and the sudden burst of exertion had sent my senses into a tailspin. Slowly, I stood up again and began to wobble the last few steps to the latrine where I squatted over the hole in the ground.

My body almost entirely emptied itself of all the foreign African food that my digestive system must have been terribly suspicious of. I had been nowhere near as cautious with my diet as I should have been before traveling into the backcountry. Now, I was paying the price for it. Every time I thought that I was finished and hesitantly stood up, more would come and I would squat back down.

With my tights around my ankles, I rubbed the goose bumps on my thighs that were raised by the frigid night air. Hovering just a few inches from the cool ground with just a little relief in my stomach and now a burning in my quads from the sustained squat, I honestly believed that this was the most miserable I had ever been in my twenty-three years on this planet. If that were not enough, when I went to finally wipe with the flimsy roll of toilet paper stolen from a hostel in Spain, I learned that some of the shit had frozen to my skin.

After returning to my tent, I would still have to make two more trips to the latrine during the night and wouldn't achieve more than two hours of continuous sleep before the morning came. The next day was important because we would make our way to base camp, Barafu, and prepare for our summit push that very evening; I was already feeling exhausted and drained.

Before we began the scramble up Barranco Wall, the near-vertical face and first obstacle out of camp, Emmanuel was approached by one of the other guides because a porter had become extremely ill.

Contrary to what I believed, there is not a doctor at all times at these camps throughout the mountain. This other guide saw my profession listed as "paramedic" when I signed into the logbook and knew that I was hiking with Emmanuel. He pleaded with Emmanuel to fetch me and asked if there was anything that I could do to help, then rushed me over to the ailing man.

Inside the tent lay an incredibly toned and athletic Tanzanian man in his mid-thirties. He was taking deep laborious breaths, looked incredibly uncomfortable clutching his chest, and a sheen of sweat shone from his brow.

Apparently in the middle of the night when I was having my own medical drama, he had woken up from his sleep with a sudden onset of chest pain and had vomited twice. They had already placed a pulse oximeter on him, which is normally carried to perform routine checks on clients, and his now read sixty-four percent. While it would be normal for someone who is not acclimatized to drop into the eighty percent range at this altitude, a porter who does this routinely should be somewhere close to normal. The device, which also measures a patient's heart rate, showed his at only thirty-four beats per minute. I checked his carotid pulse and it matched the number almost exactly.

Looking at the man who was now too weak to speak, I asked questions to his lead guide who had now informed me that the porter's parents had both died of heart attacks, and he also had some "heart problem" but was unsure of any further details. Immediately, I instructed another porter to retrieve an oxygen tank and we fixed the non-re-breather over his nose and mouth. Out of my own medical kit, I gave him some Tylenol for pain and a tab of Zofran for the nausea. Obviously concerned about a major cardiac event, I told his lead guide they needed to get the sick porter down the mountain as quickly and safely as possible. Ideally, they could carry him down to a lower camp where he could be evacuated by helicopter, but the lead guide shook his head and said that helicopters were truly only options for wealthy clients—a porter could never afford such an expense, even if it meant life or death.

A group of porters loaded the man onto a makeshift gurney, and under their own strength, they carried their friend down the mountain at an unimaginable pace along with my notes to the receiving physician, wherever they may be. The bond amongst this group of formidable men is something that can only be understood once witnessed, as it is too beautiful and powerful to describe.

Unfortunately, that wouldn't be my last experience of "playing doctor" on Kilimanjaro over the next few days. I would exhaust my own supplies treating eight different people with complaints ranging from sprained knees and ankles to acute altitude sickness. The work was not cumbersome as it was nice to feel useful, offsetting my feelings of inadequacy due to all the assistance from Emmanuel and the team of porters.

Moving upwards, the warm African sun that had accompanied us for the first few days suddenly disappeared as we headed ever closer to base camp. We walked amongst the clouds now, donning our warmer gear to protect against the plummeting temperatures. Just below Barafu camp, Emmanuel and I were assaulted by a hailstorm while crossing a boulder field. Tiny balls of ice fell relentlessly from the sky sounding like a chorus of wind chimes as they struck against the slate rocks arranged like a mosaic over the ground.

We hustled up the last steep climb to camp and quickly assembled the tents as the snow began to fall and the storm pressed on. Despite the dismal weather the feeling was surreal; at just over 15,350 feet I stood at the base camp for our summit push, which was now only hours away.

Warm tea comforted the chill that had crept over my whole body. I ate quietly in my tent while the wind whipped the weathered nylon flaps around me with a deafening roar. The excitement of the next twenty-four hours was almost uncontainable. Now it truly did feel like an adventure, the elements showcasing a small sample of what they were capable of in this environment. Thus far, the weather had been better and more enjoyable than I could have ever anticipated, but as I listened to the wind whip around my thin cocoon, it felt like we were really on a mountain.

Emmanuel and I met just after dinner for a quick summit briefing where we discussed the route, layering systems and timing. We were to wake up at midnight and begin hiking around one in the morning. Inside my tent I laid out the four layers I would have on my bottom, five on my top, two pairs of socks, neck gaiter, balaclava, winter hat, and two pairs of gloves. At six p.m. I was nestled in my sleeping bag and surprisingly fell straight to sleep, my eyes closing to the dim grey light in the tent's warm interior. Twelve hours from now, I would be standing on the highest point in Africa.

● ● ●

"Mr. Bobby, it is time." One of the porters said to me through the tent wall as I awoke from my sleep. Groggily, I removed my left arm from the sleeping bag and glanced at my wrist to see my watch read 12:02 a.m. It was cold, but the quiet was immeasurable. The wind had disappeared and the night was silent as could be.

Slowly and methodically I changed into my summit clothes and double-checked all of my gear to be sure all was in order. I had never drunk so much tea in my life, but it was a welcome comfort in the freezing temperature of the early morning air. Breakfast was quick and light as I was still worried about the fragility of my digestive tract. I attempted to shit in the latrine but could not get anything moving. It was cumbersome delayering so much just to go to the bathroom, but I would much rather do it in the shelter of these wooden walls than further up on the exposed trail to the peak. Unfortunately, we had a strict timeline to follow so I could not spend the entire morning squatting over the black and foul hole in the ground.

In the distance, a train of headlamps could be seen slowly making their way up the mountain like an endless stream of cars on the highway. The stars above them were unlike any I had seen before. They seemed so close that if you truly dreamed it possible you could simply reach out and touch them. Magic was in the air, and today was another one of those days I knew I would remember forever.

Emmanuel and I began to walk through the freshly fallen snow from the previous evenings storm, our trudge even more *pole, pole* than usual. He described the pace of our five-kilometer climb and 4,000-foot ascent to the summit as an elderly man with arthritis walking backwards. Physically, I was fine, in fact as the climb towards the stars continued I felt great despite my body's recent protest. Mentally however, I was strained. I knew it would take us five to six hours to reach Uhuru Peak, the summit of Kilimanjaro, but other than that, I had no frame of reference of how far we had come and how far was left to go. In the pitch dark of the night the only thing I could see was the small window of light in front of me from my headlamp and then the lights of others higher up, far, far, away. Snow crunched beneath me as I blindly followed ever-upward, switchback after switchback. The cold crept up from my peripheries, our movement so slow that not enough energy was being expended to generate a comfortable amount of body heat. Still, as we progressed forward, we continued to pass group after group.

Every five switchbacks I gave myself the mental reward of checking my watch to see how much time had elapsed. At two a.m. I chowed down a Cadbury chocolate bar like it was nobody's business, the joy from my taste buds sending encouragement to the rest of my body, and upward we went.

As we ascended further I began to notice splotches of various colors staining the virgin snow off the side of the trail. My curiosity forced me to stop and take a closer look—it was blood and vomit from other hikers whom had already passed and were not handling the altitude with the ease they must have hoped for. The sight and smell began to make me feel nauseous myself.

Inevitable tragedy, relatively speaking, struck at around four a.m. A very unfortunate sensation in my stomach signaled that I needed to go to the bathroom, and I needed to go soon. Pressure built and I began to squeeze my legs closer together while I walked.

"Emmanuel, I need to stop to use the bathroom."

He stopped and turned around. "Okay, go for it," he said matter-of-factly.

"No," I said. "I need to go the other kind of bathroom."

His face nodded in understanding, "Oh. Yes, there is a boulder ten minutes ahead on the left, can you hold it until then?"

I nodded my head yes, still unsure how such accurate knowledge of this mountain was possible. How did he know that? We were in the pitch dark with minimal reference points. The knowledge and expertise of the guides never ceased to impress me.

Sure enough, ten minutes later Emmanuel pointed off to the left side of the trail and motioned for me to go while he removed his thermos from his own pack for a sip of hot drink.

I shuffled off the trail and struggled to unzip, unbutton, and untie all of my layers of pants. And there I squatted, somewhere between 17,000 to 18,000 feet, wind now howling around my exposed butt as I did my business near what I now recognized as a steep drop-off.

There I was, taking the most memorable bowel movement of my life, butt cheeks frozen in the cold African air. Bet you never thought you'd see that sentence in your lifetime. Finishing up, I removed the last of my toilet paper that foresight had led me to cleverly store in the outer chest pocket of my parka for quick and easy access. Then in one strong gust of wind that almost had me off my feet, the toilet paper was gone and my gloved hand clutched at empty air. Now, I was in quite a predicament. With my butt getting colder and colder, risking frostbite to a rather sensitive area, I needed to get my bottoms back on quickly. So I did the only thing I could do; grabbing handfuls of the pure white packed snow off the ground, I wiped.

Thankfully, my stomach seemed to be held at bay after that incident and we crossed over the significant landmark of Stella Point, the first and only waypoint on the route. Situated at 18,828 feet and 0.7 kilometers from the summit, we could now turn around to the east and see the sun rising. The orange glow of the horizon highlighted the curvature of the Earth, something I had never seen before in my life. Beautiful hues of purple and light blue joined the orange light in a cloudless sky that reflected off the brilliant white of the snowy ground. You could have told me that I was in Antarctica and I would have believed you, much less so Africa. This frozen landscape was as rugged as it was beautiful and surpassed any sort of wonder I could muster.

Although we had less than a kilometer left there was still an hour of hiking to reach the true summit. That hour passed quickly as the sunlight that had softened our day into dawn now illuminated the stunning and dramatic rock formations crystalized by snow and ice. Every direction I looked in, I had a view that took my breath away; I couldn't believe it.

The famous weather-beaten brown summit sign came into view and grew larger and larger as we approached it until I could finally read the words. Slowly, I reached a gloved hand up and I touched it, feeling the rough texture of the wood underneath my well-protected hands. I did it. I was here—19,341 feet, the highest point on the African continent. To celebrate, I opened the main compartment of my summit pack and removed my Tom Brady jersey to pose for a picture. A German hiker had to crouch down and hold the bottom of the jersey to keep it still in the defiant gusts of wind.

Once all the photos had been taken and the high-fives were finished, I stepped off to the side and took a moment to myself. Closing my eyes, I muttered a quick prayer to Rachel, knowing that she was listening to me; I could feel it in my heart. Almost 20,000 feet closer to her than I usually was at sea level, I thought it would be hard for her not to hear me. As I had in Portugal, I once again had another one-sided conversation with my friend who I missed so much.

I asked her to stay with me and watch over me, and to see the magnificent places of the world through my eyes, since she no longer could. I promised her that just like in this moment, anytime I was faced with such exquisite beauty, I would speak to her again so that she could share it with me. *Why'd you do it Rach?* I wondered silently. She could have been here, she could have seen this, there was so much more to climb and conquer. The realization that I'll never truly know what she was going through presented itself once more, and with that I could feel the physical pain on the left side of my chest. I would not let the sorrow take away from the moment I was now in; Rachel would have hated that more than anything.

Turning slowly, pivoting on my heels, I took in the 360-degree view of one of the most amazing places I have ever had the privilege of standing. Emmanuel came over, hugged and congratulated me, and I him, and we both stood there and smiled. The transition from sadness to elation to what came next was like an unfortunate rollercoaster.

I stopped smiling; a feeling of dread surging through me as that terrible sensation in my stomach began again, except this time there was no boulder to hide behind. We were completely exposed, standing on the summit of the mountain in broad daylight surrounded by many other people, and it was still a long way down. The pain was not nearly as bad as it was earlier, but it was present enough for me to know what was to come.

After fifteen minutes atop Africa that I would have traded for nothing, Emmanuel gestured that we needed to begin our descent. I walked slowly, rather unsure of myself, and released a fart. But it wasn't a fart. Now I had officially accomplished something that I'm sure only an elite few can claim the prestige of doing. I shit my pants on the summit of Mount Kilimanjaro.

It was a fast but uncomfortable jaunt back down to base camp where I beelined to the latrine and used the remainder of my travel-sized baby wipes to clean myself before sliding on my only other pair of under-wear. We still had another seven miles to descend down to Mweka Camp; the day was far from over. Although I could have never imagined the circumstances of my summit day, all of the best adventures are the ones you cannot plan for. Twenty-four hours later, at an altitude of just 5,380 feet, we exited Kilimanjaro National Park through Mweka Gate, and were soon in an old beaten-down truck on our way back to Moshi. After so much time in the sweltering heat of Africa, the ocean was calling, and I knew exactly where I was going to next.

● ● ●

Mafia Island is an area covering just about 400 square kilometers off the coast of Tanzania and is home to about twenty different villages. It is often overshadowed by Zanzibar, a much more popular and touristy island to the North. In my research of places I could dive in Tanzania, the much less trafficked sites of Mafia and its resident population of juvenile whale sharks sealed the deal. I spoke to Jenny and Warren at Big Blu Dive Center in the southeastern corner of the island and arranged to stay for about two weeks.

Getting to Mafia was honestly much easier than I imagined. After a sweaty and uncomfortable layover in the Dar es Salaam Airport, a small bush plane carried me and five other passengers thirty minutes over the Indian Ocean to the extraordinarily small airport on the island. I breathed in the same humid air that had smothered me in the city that morning, this time improved by the gentle island breeze and the salty tinge that came with it.

A large African man handed me my backpack and I walked from the runway to the main airport building one hundred meters away. Three employees greeted me in English and had me sign into the entry book on the counter; I was the only American to come to the island in at least the past several days. Many of the others before me were from various European countries with a scattering of Aussies and Kiwis, but the common denominator between us was the "reason for visit" column: diving.

An islander working for Big Blu flagged me down and motioned me over to an old white van with the dive center insignia stickered to the windshield. The twenty-minute ride from the airport revealed a scene which perfectly matched my imagination's image of a typical African island community. Men, women, and children bustled through the village streets with large baskets of fruit carried on their heads, freshly caught fish lay filleted on ice in store fronts, and the salty smell of the nearby ocean tingled around my nostrils. We pulled into Big Blu and I was comforted by the sturdy straw-roofed structures that brought back fond memories of Rancho Esperanza.

I was greeted enthusiastically and with open arms by the staff and was quickly handed a large coconut with a colorful straw poking out the top. *My God,* I thought to myself, *I think that I am on a vacation.* For the next two weeks I would have no stress of travel, no mountains to climb or races to run. It would just be me, the ocean, some beer, and a whole island to explore. A young woman showed me to the safari tent that would be my home on the island. Unpacking my bag, the air grew thick and oppressive around me in the close quarters of the army green nylon. Instead of exploring first, I would quickly need to arrange tomorrow's dives and then go for a long swim in the very inviting ocean to cool off.

After all the correspondence over email, I finally met Jenny, one of the dive masters at Big Blu, who greeted me just as amicably as the rest of the staff. We set up two dives for the next day, and less than ten minutes later, I was swimming in the crystal-clear warm waters off the beach, mere footsteps from the dive center. The turquoise oasis that had become my new playground was the most relaxing thing I had experienced in months. Looking out to sea, I saw the old Arab dhows that were fashioned into dive boats bobbing lightly in the gentle waves. Turning around toward the shore, the beach spread about a quarter mile to the south and was dotted with palm trees on the light-colored sand with hammocks strung between them. It was a paradise untouched by the commercialism of my normal world, and there was no place I would rather be.

For solo travelers, dinner was communal, allowing me to meet and chat with divers from all walks of life, and places I had never traveled to before. I quickly became friends with Karin and Marc from Austria, and Magnus and Ann of Sweden, both couples that have enjoyed diving all over the world. We dined on fresh and perfectly seasoned fish and octopus, all caught the same day, while chatting about dive sites in corners of the world I had never heard of. Jenny, Warren, Abou, and all the other dive masters at Big Blu ate with us and described the different spots around the island and what we could expect to see. The biodiversity in Tanzania's only protected marine park was a diver's heaven.

Days blurred into each other with the same routine repeated, but I didn't mind the regularity as I was quite literally living the dream. Diving amazing sites, eating fresh and delicious food, swimming in tropical waters, reading in a hammock, and meeting new, like-minded people each and every day. Spritzed into that mix were magical afternoons snorkeling with whale sharks and visiting nearby smaller islands to watch the hatching of baby sea turtles. Coming to Africa with the primary focus of completing a marathon and move closer towards my continents goal now seemed to be an afterthought. That is, until one night at dinner when I had a peculiar conversation with Magnus.

Many of my new friends who I had been diving, eating, and drinking with nightly knew that I was a runner of sorts, but I had not revealed my goal of completing the continents to them. I tended to keep that to myself as it always gravitates back towards the marathon bombing, and I did not want that to spoil this immaculate paradise for me.

"So Bobby," Magnus said while he swallowed a large bite of white fish, "which of your races has been your favorite?"

This question I had been familiar with responding to many, many times over the past few years, and since the previous January, my answer had remained unchanged. "Well," I spoke slowly and finished chewing the mango in my mouth, "Antarctica was a good one." I smiled as the words left my mouth. This is generally an answer people don't expect simply because they never knew a race on the most desolate continent on earth even existed.

"Antarctica!" Magnus half gasped and half laughed. "You're joking! They have such a thing? What was it like?" The others nodded in agreement of his inquiry, waiting for my next words.

I took another bite of mango from my plate, a grin spreading across my face. "It was a little bit colder than here!" We all laughed.

In brief detail I described the glaciers, penguins, and polar plunge, emphasizing mostly that it was a special race to me because it was in an area of the world that humans had not yet destroyed. When I finished my soliloquy I looked back at Magnus and he was smiling at me.

"If you enjoy running in places where many others do not, then maybe you should run a marathon here?" His strong Scandinavian accent added a sense of power to his question.

This got everyone at the table chatting and nodding in agreement. Of the Big Blu staff at the table, none had ever heard of a marathon being mapped and completed on the island before, so I would be the first one. Hell, it might even mean winning a marathon for the first time!

Technically, I was supposed to get some sort of long run in while on the island to prepare for an ultra marathon in New York shortly upon my return to the United States, and this would be a good excuse to get it done. Without thinking too much of the heat, humidity, and unknown logistics I announced to the table, "Okay, I'll do it." Everybody clapped.

The next day before my first dive, I laced up my shoes to see how much the equatorial climate would truly affect my ability to run. My answer came when I found myself drenched in sweat from the effort of getting dressed and stretching before I had even taken a step. After six painful miles, with the tropical sun pounding down on my glaringly un-pigmented skin, I had to rethink my strategy. Of the many challenges I would face trying to complete this race, those that concerned me the most were staying hydrated and protecting myself from heatstroke.

Beneath the ocean that day, as I cruised around the reefs, my mind was elsewhere, churning over the logistics of making the "Mafia Island Marathon" a reality. About thirty minutes into the dive, I noticed a shadow passing slowly over the sandy bottom, and a foreign feeling of coolness in the water ran up my spine, causing my hair to stand up on end. A storm was forecast to come in that day and the clouds were just starting to roll in, completely obscuring the sun. The sun...If the sun wasn't out, the heat would be much more bearable. I couldn't plan on a storm coming every day, but I could count on the sun falling below the horizon at a very specific time each day. Nighttime. I would run my solo race at night.

Thunder cracked and rain pelted the cloth covering the dhow as we sailed back towards Big Blu. The rhythmic beating of the raindrops sent me into a trance-like state while I thought of the other obstacle: hydration. Pleased at the idea of running at nighttime to avoid the heat, I knew there had to be a solution close at hand.

One suggestion was to cache bottled water around the island at certain checkpoints, but I would have to do that during the day, and while the water sat in the afternoon sun, it would become hot and foul. There was also the risk of islanders taking the bottles, not knowing what they were for and how important they would be to me in the middle of a long, lonely night.

That's when being a little bit of a fraidy-cat about running alone at night on a foreign island put the answer I needed right into my lap. Instead of doing 13.1 miles out and back, I would run a series of loops in different directions that I could map on my Garmin GPS watch, never leaving me too far from my home base. At the entrance to Big Blu I could leave a whole stash of water, snacks, extra headlamp batteries, and mosquito repellant.

At dinner that night I announced my intentions to attempt the marathon in the wee hours of the morning of the following day, which just happened to be St. Patrick's Day. Everyone wished me luck and told me I was on my own; they'd congratulate me with a beer when they woke up for breakfast after the sun rose.

My stomach quivered with a jittery feeling when I went back to my tent and laid out all of my food, water, and running clothes. This wasn't the normal nervousness experienced around the crowded start line, with pre-race music blaring through the speakers and a large digital countdown clock. Instead it was the nervousness encountered by having to run alone for a few hours lit only by a headlamp, over a route that even I wasn't yet sure of, on a remote island off the coast of Africa. I had no idea Dr. Seuss meant something like this when he first inspired me with *Oh, the Places You'll Go!*

I looked at my watch: 2100. In four hours, my alarm would ring and I would begin another one of my grand ideas, although I wasn't sure how grand this one really was. The more I thought about it, the more I felt this was something I'd be happy about once it was in the past, but living the moment of it, not so much. To ease the mental checklist required at my 1:15 a.m. start, I slept in my running clothes, sheets thrown off as the humidity still pressed close, even after dark.

Only fifteen minutes had passed of me lying restlessly in bed, my mind traveling in a million different directions about what the morning would bring. Most of the thoughts were negative and my head began to spin with anxiety. There was no possible way I'd be able to sleep tonight, my mind already spiraling down a now well-known path of escalating stimulation. But this was my race, there was no official start time, I did not need to wait for a starting pistol to go off. Screw it; I'm going to start right now.

Before I could change my mind, I got out of bed, rolled my socks up over my ankles, put my headlamp around my hat, my shoes on my feet, and unzipped the tent door with an arm full of snack crackers and water bottles. My legs floated over the ground toward the exit of Big Blu like I was in a dream. A sense of relief flooded through my body, charged with the knowledge that I was off to make it happen and would not have to toss and turn through a sleepless pre-race night.

Carefully, I balanced my bottles and snacks on Big Blu's roughly painted welcome sign at the end of the driveway. Dirt crunched under my shoes that had now endured the beating of a trail race in England, a boring marathon in Tanzania, and climbed to the summit of Kilimanjaro, all within the past six weeks.

The moon was bright but the visibility down the road leading north was still minimal under the stream of light coming from my headlamp. Foreign sounds chimed loudly from the surrounding trees while the jungle came to life under the cover of night. Mosquitoes and other flying insects frequented the newly artificial light that I was creating and just as quickly, large bats would swoop down to feast on them right in front of my face.

Turns out, the bats would be my biggest audience during this event with their screeches a substitute for the screams and applause of thousands of people. The incredible numbers of them that swooped through the pitch-black night on Mafia Island made the noise level almost indistinguishable from that of a roaring audience.

One foot in front of the other, I ran two miles out until I was turned around by the familiar chirping of my Garmin watch. I was uneasy with the unfamiliar sounds and surroundings, but I knew this could be done if I maintained the mental resilience to just push through and grind it out. It was while having this internal pep talk with myself that the thought hit me: I had been so disappointed by the lack of adventure during the Kilimanjaro Marathon that this race was now making up for everything that it was deficient in. My newly founded Mafia Island Marathon was scary, weird, and different, a true adventure! It was just what I wanted and delivered to me in a way I never would have dreamed.

But that's how most of our greatest memories and adventures happen. They are the ones we can't plan for or anticipate, they are spontaneous and wild, beyond the reach of your normal imagination and only able to be truly realized in the moment they are happening.

My pulse surged and adrenaline pumped through my veins at this new recognition that I was living out exactly what I had hoped for. Through the night I ran this way and that, out and back, loops, and everything in between. I ran to places I'm sure I would not recognize come daylight and smiled wider and wider as the mileage count on my Garmin moved ever upward.

At twenty-five miles, I turned back down the driveway of Big Blu and jogged my way through the main building and onto the sandy beach that I frequented during the hot sun in the daylight hours. Moonlight shone on the dark water, the waves lapped softly against the shore, and the salty air filled my nose and pressed against my tongue. My senses were alive as I turned off my headlamp and ran on the beach by moonlight now in the early hours of St. Patrick's Day. Having initially wanted this run to be over and done with to reflect upon in the past, my spirit felt intensely alive and content in the present moment, running wild.

As much as I can describe what it was like to be on that beach under the shining bright moon in a far off land, finishing something no one had ever done before, it feels impossible to truly share that experience. That moment belonged to me and only me, and for that reason it was magical and special in a way I had never felt before. In front of a crowd of no one, my watch clicked 26.2 miles and I threw my arms high above my head, smiling to the inky night sky. It now felt like I had run the marathon I had needed and wanted from this continent. Africa had gifted me with an experience that was running and adventure in its purest form.

Sweaty, exhausted, but fulfilled, I made my way to the shower stall, once again guided by my headlamp. The cool water washed the sweat from my tense muscles and I reveled in the sensation of relief. After a few minutes of glory, I turned the water off and spun around to the wooden door where my towel hung. A small yelp escaped my mouth before I cut it off with my hand. There, looking back at me on a shelf about the height of my chest, stared a fist-sized brown spider. Even the rough and tough hairy adventurer can still have the wits scared out of him by an oversized furry arachnid.

My time in Africa was still not finished after I departed from one of the most amazing islands I had ever visited. The year prior I had met a dive guide in Iceland named Richard Leckie who ended up becoming a very good friend. Coincidentally he was now working in South Africa, so naturally it made sense to go visit to get some more diving in and catch up with him. Thus, I joyously continued my diving vacation in the rich waters of the African coast. Although Richard was a friend I had only known briefly, his free spirit and kind soul allowed for an impactful connection shared amongst travelers. These types of friendships have blessed me around the world and provided so much meaning to my life.

Returning home to the United States from Africa was a more difficult transition back to "the real world" than many of my prior travels. As far as culture and exposure to poverty and undeveloped land, this trip far surpassed all the others. The thought I kept returning to was, *I was only there for two and a half months, how is Ryan going to fit back into society in the United States after two and a half years?*

Most people will never have the opportunity, or maybe the desire, to travel to Africa. After being lucky enough to experience the beauty and tough lessons of this continent, I felt very aware of this lack of opportunity for others. I thought that perhaps by speaking about and bringing the experience to people as best I could, I could try to share some of what can be learnt from exposure to the "other" that is traveling in developing countries. So that's what I did, starting with a local high school. By highlighting the work Ryan is doing in Rwanda to high school students soon to be headed towards university and important life decisions, maybe I could inspire others to be more mindful of the world as a whole and not just the small bubble they live in. Most importantly, I could help expose them to a better and more realistic view of the world; one that the United States is not the center of. Countries are just lines drawn on a map. Those invented borders, however, create immense divisions that continue to hold back the development of many nations. As Americans we certainly have an important role to play on the international stage, and have a lot to offer the world. Sometimes, however, it's more important to recognize what the world can offer and teach us, something only available if we open ourselves up to it, and transcend the bubble we place ourselves in back home. It was with this motivation and context of global empathy that I spoke of Ryan's incredible sacrifice and unparalleled dedication to helping others in less fortunate circumstances.

The more I reflect on my time in Africa, the more I am reminded that the importance of my journey was not the marathons or the mountains. Time and time again I left the United States to run races to move closer towards the goal of completing the seven continents, and every single trip showed me that the race itself was such an insignificant part of the experience. It is the lessons learned, friends made, and memories had by the travel that hold the most important part in healing my heart and soul. Running was just the vessel that got me to where I needed to be to make it all happen. At this point, five continents down and four years removed from the marathon bombing, the trauma that had motivated my mission was now little more than an afterthought at times.

After having my moment on top of Kilimanjaro, being as geographically close to Rachel as I ever had, I knew pieces of me still needed to be fixed. My time in nature was generally where I could trust to put myself back together, but how could I now? The very mountains that I would be returning to for my training for the last two continents were the places I had spent the most time with Rachel. I found it a bit ironic really, that while in the middle of such an epic journey I would come close to resolving one major emotional hurdle only to almost immediately have another placed before me.

I knew the months ahead would be painful, but as with so many times before, the only direction to move was forward. Now looking towards the summer in what used to be my place of peace and serenity, I feared what emotion the White Mountains of New Hampshire would unearth for me this time.

CHAPTER EIGHT

WILD

Torres del Paine, Chile
September 2017

t was with some disbelief that I began to turn my thoughts towards the final two marathons of my seven continents journey. To fund these next two adventures, I continued to work any and every open shift I could. I spent many of my days on long, tranquil runs, conditioning my legs, while my nights were filled with the lights and sirens of the ambulance blaring on the way to an emergency. These were the two pillars of my life now: work and training. To save as much as possible for my next big adventure I continued to reside in my car while banking as much overtime as possible. For the first time, I discovered that the benefits of working nightshift included providing me with a place to stay, even if I couldn't sleep. Wherever I was, the majority of my time was spent daydreaming about being somewhere far, far away.

My imagination ran wild researching races through beautiful mountains in South America and Asia, but the giddiness of these plans was tainted with the knowledge that I would have to revisit the White Mountains to train. This saddened me deeply. I have never felt like I *had* to go to the mountains, it was always something that was a privilege and a joy, not something I dreaded. Rachel's death changed this for me, and I resented her for it.

As the snow thawed in New England that spring, instead of allowing the feeling of excitement for running in the mountains envelop me, I shrunk away from the feeling. Even the thought of the mountains scared me. In what had once been a place for me to reflect and heal during troubled times in my life, now lived the memories of a time I could never relive. I feared that the mountains would only bring sorrow as they stirred up recollections of the countless hikes with Rachel and the promises she had made to me of hikes we would do this year. I felt the need to go on my own. So that is what I did, and it was hard. Many times out of the blue the reality that she was gone would hit and I would cry alone on the trail. I would yell at her, ask her why, and kick at the dirt. But it would pass, and the only way to move forward was up the mountain.

In some ways, the emotional pain motivated me to achieve physical exhaustion to the point where I just wouldn't feel at all. It was an odd, sadistic style of training, that wasn't ineffective from a pure fitness perspective. Mentally, some days were better than others. I moved slowly closer to accepting the unchangeable reality that I really had completed my last hike with Rachel. I also attempted to let myself sit with the knowledge that I will never have the answers to the questions I seek. Even though it was difficult more times than not, I diligently returned to the Whites several times a week. Although at first motivated by my physical training, over time I began to once more feel the powerful pull of the mountains I had loved so much. They were still there for me as a place of peace, and of real connection between my mind, my body, and the world around me. As the summer passed by, I did begin to heal. Instead of living in the past, I realized that these stark granite peaks were the closest I could feel to Rachel now and forever. My feet moved over the ground knowing that Rachel's boots had at one time passed over these same stones. She would always be with me while I hiked in these mountains and I simply had to take comfort in that. Thankfully so, because these mountains were the perfect training ground to build my legs in preparation for Chilean Patagonia.

● ● ●

When I was in Chile the first time, with Marathon Adventures, even as I was running the Punta Arenas race, I thought, *Is this what I really want? Running laps up and down a city street, just to say my feet carried me 26.2 miles on this specific location in the world?* It didn't settle well with me, and a feeling of hidden relief had swept over me when the race had ended prematurely. At first it felt like a waste, that I had thrown away an opportunity to finish sooner, but I realized that was not how I wanted *my* seven continent marathon journey to go. I did gain something from the first trip down to Chile in January 2016. My German roommate from that same venture, Matthias, and another friend, Nancy, decided to take a trip to Torres del Paine National Park with me on my twenty-second birthday. This dramatic corner of Chilean Patagonia was a place I had never heard of at the time, but now a place I would be distraught to ever forget.

The immense beauty of the park that summer day in January drew me in as if it had its own unique and powerful gravity. Magnificent granite towers soared into the cloudless blue sky, masking the treachery of an unrelenting wind. Lush valleys and bright turquoise lakes lay in the shadow of stunningly high peaks. No matter which way you turned, the view gazed upon could have been a spread in *National Geographic*. That holiday made a huge impression on my excitable mind; I felt as though everything was happening for a reason and that I was destined to return to this park.

Upon my return to the United States, I wasted no time in trying to make sure that vision was realized and immediately began to search for races within Torres del Paine. Ultra Trail Torres del Paine greeted me at the very top of my Google search. They did not offer a marathon, but they did entice runners to challenge the fifty-kilometer course, something I did not think twice about.

Brains have a funny way of working. In an endurance event, they concentrate and focus so much on the task at hand that you couldn't imagine pushing farther or longer than what you anticipated to do before you started. Well, until it's over. Then it's what's longer, what's harder, what's faster?

Before my first marathon, I would have never expected to run further than that, until I finished it. And before my first fifty kilometers, I was certain that would be the furthest I would ever run, until I finished that one too. But the idea for a fifty-miler first took hold with the age-old aide of peer pressure.

When looking at my race calendar for 2017, I had an inkling that I would be able to complete the seven continents this year. After returning from Africa, I would have five months to toy around with other personal goals before traveling again to Chile to resume the continent pursuit. Amongst those were a second Ironman and to increase my racing distance to fifty miles, a feat arguably undesirable to me, so I consulted a friend whom I knew would push me in the right direction.

Joanna Marczyk is a phenomenal runner and even better friend who I met while studying and running at Saint Anselm College. We ran cross country together briefly before she graduated, then she skipped the marathon distance altogether and delved straight into trail runs of fifty kilometers. Knowing she had wanted to bridge the gap to the next distance, I sent out a text to see if she'd be up for making an attempt in early 2017. She replied with a resounding, "Yes!"

We signed up for the fifty-miler in the North Face Endurance Challenge at Bear Mountain in New York. It was mid-May, about five weeks after my return from Africa. When April came around faster than either of us expected, I realized how incredibly underprepared I was for a potential fifty-mile jaunt the following month. Thankfully, Jo was as well and she didn't shame me when I asked if she was interested in dropping down to the fifty kilometer race instead.

Bailing on the fifty miler remained a nagging presence, consistently bothering me when it popped in to my head. Apparently it was eating at Jo too, because I had a stupid idea at the beginning of the summer that I texted her about: let's do the fifty miler at Ultra Trail Torres del Paine, this being the first year they had ever offered the distance.

Once again, she entertained the idea with an emphatic, "Yes!"

As September drew closer and closer I started to truly wonder how you train for a fifty-mile race through the mountains of Patagonia. I wasn't sure because I was too afraid what I would find out if I Googled it. A few weeks before the event, the organizers sent out the required medical forms necessary to compete in the race. One of the forms concernedly asked for my blood type in case a severe emergency occurred.

An additional requisite was the signature of a physician to medically clear me fit to run. Unfortunately, funding months of international travel necessitates working just about every day. This left absolutely zero opportunity for me to make an appointment to see my doctor to have the form signed, especially considering that it was sent only two weeks before the race. Naturally, and probably irresponsibly, I decided to treat these forms like a school field trip permission slip and forge a doctor's signature. The event being in another country made the likelihood of any sort of verification incredibly low. Additionally, the messy handwriting of a doctor is probably the easiest thing to counterfeit.

With my bags packed and double-checked, I drove to Jo's apartment in Connecticut the night before our one a.m. flight out of New York City. We preemptively prepped for our early hours departure so we could go out to enjoy a few beers before the flight; priorities resolutely in check.

I was glad we had it all squared away considering the extent of packing and preparation needed for such an adventure. We weren't only running the race on our trip to Chilean Patagonia, but we were also planning a five-day trek on a hiking route known as the "W" in Torres del Paine National Park. With winter still lingering in the Southern Hemisphere, specifically in a place home to some of the wildest weather on the planet, our pack weights were anything but light. Cold weather gear, rain gear, specialized tents, sleeping bags, and cooking supplies were added to our relatively weightless running apparel. The sixty-mile hike would be how we spent the precious last days before our first fifty-mile trail race.

● ● ●

We arrived at the Singing Lamb Hostel in Puerto Natales nearly twenty-seven hours after our plane left the runway in New York. It was a brisk, windy day in Southern Chile as snowflakes gently descended from the sky. After taking the always pleasant, post-wicked-long-travel-day shower, we took to the streets to book some of the campsites necessary for our trek through Torres.

The online booking system through the few Chilean companies that owned the sites in the park was frustrating, complicated, and inoperable. Since it was the low season, booking in the town of Puerto Natales wouldn't be an issue. In the high season, reservations would have to be made upwards of six months in advance; pretty crazy for a park that sees fewer visitors in a year than Yosemite receives during one week in the summer.

In broken Spanish and utilizing multiple hand gestures, we completed our task and continued onward through town to seek out a pizza place that I found on TripAdvisor called La Guanaca. Because of the exceptional service, amazing pisco sours, and surprisingly delicious pizza, this would be where we ate dinner every single night we spent in Puerto Natales.

Unfortunately, unlike our dinner, the weather at the start of the week was not as wonderful; in fact it looked absolutely miserable. Because of this we pushed back the start of our hike, leaving us an extra day to explore in town. While we sat in the hostel room scouring websites and guidebooks for something to do, I had Google Maps open to gauge how far apart various locations were. Then, a red dotted line on the right side of the screen caught my eye. It was the border of Chile and Argentina, and it appeared close—really close.

"How do you feel about running to Argentina?" I asked sheepishly. "Check out how close this is."

Jo took my phone from me and a big smile began to grow across her face. "Are you serious? I am so down!"

The border was approximately eighteen kilometers from our hostel, making for a total thirty-six kilometer run roundtrip. We both reasoned that it wouldn't be the smartest decision to run the whole loop the day before starting a five-day hike that would then lead into a fifty-mile race. Instead, we would take a taxi to within five kilometers of the border, run over, and return making for a fourteen to fifteen-mile run. Two aspects of our plan were foreseen to be slightly challenging.

First, explaining to a taxi driver (in Spanish) that we wanted to be dropped off just before a country border was suspicious at best. Second, although we were perfectly innocent, two Americans showing up at border patrol on foot wearing only running clothes and small packs isn't necessarily your everyday occurrence. Regardless, we checked out of our hostel that morning with high aspirations: to cross borders and avoid detainment.

Needing a new place to stay for when we returned from our run, we wandered a mile to a different hostel. I had noticed it when we were exploring Puerto Natales the previous day and the name, Wild, had immediately drawn my eye. One of the owners cordially greeted us, nodded skeptically when we explained our plans for the day, but still let us stash our bags until we could check in later that afternoon.

Now, armed with running packs full of rain gear, we made our way over to the taxi office. We were ready to cross some borders.

● ● ●

"¿Es possible que tomar un taxi aquí?" I asked with a miserable American accent as I handed them my phone. On the phone was a screenshot of Google Maps with a pin dropped five kilometers before the Argentinian border. We stood cramped in the crowded local taxi office, chilled from the unrelenting draft that penetrated the thin walls.

The ensuing conversation was chaotic, comical, and confusing. At one point, six taxi company employees thronged into the tiny corner office trying to comprehend the nature of my request and continued to ask why we wanted to be dropped off on the side of the road in the middle of nowhere.

Finally, a new face entered the room and handed me his phone with Google Translate already open. Trying to think of the best way to explain this, I wrote the following:

"Sorry for the confusion. We are running journalists from the United States filming a documentary with our GoPros about running through Southern Chile and Patagonia. We are looking to be dropped off just before the Argentinian border to have the opportunity to run across for our footage."

When I handed the phone back, an immediate sense of understanding washed over the readers face. "¡Sí, sí, sí!" he exclaimed and explained it to all the others in the room who let out a communal "ahhhh!" as sudden comprehension washed over the crowd of workers.

The twenty-minute drive was mostly quiet, the silence finally broken by the driver when he pulled off to the side of the road in the middle of a wide plain and asked, "¿Bien?" I nodded my head yes and handed him some Chilean pesos with a generous tip for his willingness in honoring such an odd request.

I shook out my legs as the taxi drove back towards Chile, growing smaller and smaller as it sped off into the wide-open, desert-like plain. The wind was surprisingly mild given the intensity it can reach here, but the winter air still nipped our exposed faces. In every direction, snowcapped peaks erupted from the earth like a magnificent fence at the ends of the stark fields surrounding us. With the beep of my Garmin, we were off.

The purity and simplicity of the running was everything I could have dreamed of when I began my quest to put meaning behind running again after the marathon bombing. We were running in one of the most beautiful places in the entire world, and we were alone. No other humans, no buildings, no polluted air, or loud noises; just the mountains, the wind, and our thoughts. Everything in this moment was perfect, simple, and easy.

What we didn't anticipate was passing through *two* border checkpoints because we would have to first emigrate from Chile before entering Argentina. The border agent was comically lackadaisical and couldn't seem to care less about what Jo and I were up to. We were not searched or questioned, simply allowed to pass through without a second thought.

On approaching the Argentinian border, we entered the immigration building and stood at the back of the line. As we waited, the biggest thing that stuck out to us was the freshly printed "Wanted" poster plastered on all of the windows. A grungy-looking Argentinian named Santiago was at large and in the area. I was unable to finish reading the bulletin because an agent called to us from the booth. She greeted us with a nice smile and I explained our intentions to her of simply running around in Argentina for an hour or so, and then we would return to Chile. With a puzzled look on her face, she turned to one of her colleagues and spoke words I could not hear. They both laughed and looked us up and down, and then she graciously motioned for our passports. Just like that, we had made it to Argentina.

We exited the building and then asked the most important question of the day: how short a time is it acceptable to stay in a country before exiting?

Jo and I had a brief discussion that we would try to spend an hour over the border. There was only one road and the nearest town, which was eighteen kilometers away, was definitely out of reach for us considering the additional eighteen kilometers to return back to our hostel in Puerto Natales.

As we ran down the muddy gravel path deeper into Argentina's countryside, every single car that passed us beeped multiple times. I like to think they were friendly beeps, but it was impossible to tell in what was one of the oddest experiences of my life. We took an ample amount of photos and admired the stillness of an area rarely experienced on foot. Most of all, we took the time to reflect and appreciate the unique moment we were in.

So often people come up with an idea that seems sort of ridiculous and they don't act on it for that very reason; something small, not necessarily life-changing but something that could certainly be life-enhancing, that is neglected because it is too much work, too complicated, or too odd. Seizing these opportunities and striving to break the monotony of everyday life is vital to attaining happiness. Adventure and spontaneity is what brings a smile to my soul and allows me to live without the regret of ever having to wonder, *What if?*

After thirty minutes, we turned around and headed back towards the border. Never tiring of the countless mountainous peaks in our periphery we continued on, thankfully with no appearances from Santiago, the convict on the loose.

Once again, the same border agent greeted us kindly as I told her how beautiful Argentina was. She laughed, presumably because we had seen virtually none of her country. When I look back, it is pretty wild to have been in a country and not to have eaten, or even peed, while there.

She stamped our passports and we began the short run back on the loose gravel path to the checkpoint for immigration into Chile, where we filled out our customs forms for the second time in the past three days. And just like that, our passports were stamped and our running shoes dug back into the Chilean soil. In a matter of two hours, our passports had gained four stamps, something I would not have imagined achieving in my life.

Rain began to fall lightly on the way back down Ruta 9 towards Puerto Natales. The familiar sound of beeping car horns welcomed us as they whizzed by on the route that I'm sure was rarely run on. A sign on the side of the road even read, "Ruta del Fin del Mundo"—route to the end of the world.

The landscape certainly appeared to validate the signs claim. Aside from the occasional farm, until we reached Puerto Natales there was really nothing at all. Just fields, streams, and mountains in the distance, the emptiness stunningly beautiful in its own stark nature.

Over an hour later, as the rain started to increase in intensity, the first glimpse of Puerto Natales greeted us as we crested a short but steadily graded hill. We regained our bearings thanks to the magnificent giant sloth statue at the rotary. Shortly thereafter, we swung open the door to Wild, buzzing from our fantastic, mini-adventure, an over fifteen-mile run across two countries. How often is it that you need your passport for a long run?

Jari and his wife, Demaris, the owners of Wild, waved us into the hostel out of the cold and rain. "You're crazy!" he said pulling me in for a handshake and hug before moving onto Jo. "Who does that for fun!?" he exclaimed.

They checked us in and Jari's daughter, Isa, and her boyfriend, Josh, showed us to the dorm beds upstairs.

Aside from Rancho Esperanza, Wild was by far the nicest and most welcoming hostel I have ever stayed at anywhere in the world. It wasn't just that there was free Wi-Fi, running water, heat, and no bugs; it was the people and the atmosphere that those people created. Jari and Demaris continued to reaffirm for me a hypothesis that I had developed over the last few years of traveling. You could be in a fantastic, incredible place, but with a bunch of jerks it is a miserable experience. Contrarily, the presence of interesting, soulful, and altruistic people can create an unbelievable atmosphere even in the most dire of places. Thankfully, in Patagonia we were blessed with amazing people in a magical place. These special microclimates of circumstance can never be recreated, and would be entirely different if even one piece were to be removed. Every person was an integral part of what made the dynamic special, the people and not the place that brought me the sense of new horizons and fulfillment that I searched for on my travels.

The vibe of Wild was one that brought out the creative and humanitarian side of those immersed in it. The conversations and beers shared with Jari, Josh, Demaris, and Isa throughout our time in Puerto Natales felt like an antidote to the negativity and ignorance that feels so prominent in the world right now. Pure, soulful, and simple, it was a place I felt I never wanted to leave.

With our bags and heaps of rain gear packed, we awoke before six a.m. the next morning to walk to the bus. This would bring us over the long road into Torres del Paine to begin our pre-race hike. Having previously only spent a single day in the park and marking it in my brain as one of the most beautiful places I had ever seen, my excitement was next level. Lugging our trekking packs into the undercarriage of the bus, the thought of trekking there for five whole days fixed a permanent smile to my face. I was so excited that I obviously immediately fell asleep for the majority of the ride north. A hand grasping and shaking my shoulder suddenly disturbed my sleep. It was Jo with a wide-eyed grin pointing out the window saying one word, "Guanaco!"

Guanacos are arguably some of the coolest animals on the planet, and the largest population of them in the world lived right in the heart of Torres del Paine. They are similar to a llama but possess a feisty South American attitude. Not actually, they're really quite docile. Gorgeous reddish-brown coats adorn their stoic and majestic figure. The guanaco quickly became Jo's spirit animal and a constant topic of conversation for the remainder of the trip.

After another bus, and then a ferry ride, we arrived at Paine Grande where we pitched our tent before beginning our hike in the now downpouring rain and hurricane-like gusts. Welcome to the end of the winter season in Patagonia.

The first day of trekking up to Glacier Grey was considerably the worst weather we faced on the entire five-day hike. Because of the early season, many of the camping sites were not open, forcing us to form a plan to hike the "W" in a modified fashion. This made the first day a very soggy and very cold out and back route to complete the western branch of the "W."

Oftentimes, writing short creative stories in elementary school, I would pen the statement, "the wind howled as..." Legitimately this time, the wind actually howled. It was absolute madness, forcing us to seek shelter when the gusts became dangerous. That wind pushed the rain into our faces with a speed that damaged our exposed cheeks and impaired our vision if we looked anywhere but straight down. Every so often, when the rain would stop and the winds would cease, it was suddenly impossible to decide which direction to look, as everywhere we turned was absolutely stunning: glaciers ahead of us, snowcapped peaks to the right, lush green valley behind, and a shimmering turquoise lake to our left. But just as quickly as the wild weather stopped, it would start again, and we would bow our heads, grinding onwards against the elements. These are the adventures I dreamed of and hoped for every waking second when in the comfort of my home and my "regular life." In that moment, adrenaline and dopamine surged through our veins, an intoxicating rush of thrill and pure happiness.

Moving briskly through the unrelenting gusts, we fought to reach Glacier Grey before our turn-around time. Moving through a storm like this in the dark on the slippery and heavily root covered trail would be less than ideal. Before we knew it, we rounded the bend to find ourselves face to face with the glacier; the foreground contained a sea of ice, scattered in chunks and icebergs bigger than most suburban homes in the U.S. The deep hues that adorned the underside of the larger icebergs conjured up fond memories of my time spent in Antarctica. That most beautiful shade of blue, radiating from these immense chunks of ice was undoubtedly my favorite color in the world.

I took as many photos as I could before the wind and rain numbed my hands and became too much to tolerate. Jo and I were pushing the daylight hours and needed to begin the slog back to our now-soaked tent. Just as the darkness encroached on us, we entered the valley where we had started the trail at the beginning of the day. Headlamps were only needed for the last fifteen minutes, signifying a perfectly executed timing to the day.

A huge benefit of this camp was the enclosed cooking area close by which allowed us to hang our wet clothes inside. Our new warm layers felt like heaven while we cooked our dinner and let our drenched layers dry, although I wasn't convinced they ever would. Bags of freeze-dried meals tasted gourmet after the long and taxing day and I boiled a pot of hot water to mix up some hot chocolate. An Asian man came over and asked if he could borrow my lighter to start his stove.

"Absolutely man. Here ya go." I handed him the lighter and was trying to pick up his accent. It wasn't Chinese, Japanese, and didn't even really sound Korean to me either.

When he walked back over to return the lighter I introduced myself and asked where he was from.

He chuckled a bit and said, "Well, I can tell where you're from so you may find this interesting. I'm from North Korea." I couldn't hide my surprise.

"Wow! No way. I don't mean to be insensitive, but I have never met a North Korean before!"

The man laughed again. "That's the reaction I usually get. There aren't too many of us out and about."

I probably had about a million questions for him but was trying incredibly hard not to overload him. He appeared to be in his late twenties or early thirties. He was short, with neat black hair and a modest amount of facial hair that covered his cheeks and around his mouth. Most of his gear looked new and he traveled with a sophisticated Nikon camera.

"Have you been in Torres a long time?" I asked.

"No, I just arrived two days ago. This rain has really been an unfortunate obstacle. My rain jacket is not the greatest!" He held up a sopping piece of polyester blend material but still maintained a smile on his face.

"Yeah, it was super wet out there today," I replied. "Will you be hiking for long?"

His head bobbed in an excited nod. "Yes, about another week here and then onto Argentina. This part of the world is very beautiful!"

As the night went on he proceeded to tell me how he had been traveling for the past eight months, all over the world on some exemption he had received to leave his own country. He described the miserable state of affairs in his homeland and how most of the people are generally good, stuck in a frustrating dictatorship from which they have no escape. We talked for over an hour about his travels and how fortunate he was to be able to actually get out and see the world.

I shared my hot chocolate with him and appreciated this moment for one of the many small but more memorable moments in traveling. In the midst of a highly tense situation between our countries, this was pretty incredible. In the middle of remote Chile, an American and a North Korean sat together and shared a drink, chatting about life by the heat of a camp stove. Things like this truly put into perspective the hate and animosity generated by the divisions of politics and world leaders.

The weather improved as the days went on, allowing Jo and I to enjoy the unparalleled beauty of the park with less difficulty. Chilean Patagonia is up there with those places in the world that I would return to again and again. Paying for trips is such a large investment, so I always try to travel to new places, but the pure magic of the land here had an unrelenting grasp on my heart.

Over our time in Torres del Paine, many other hikers told us about the magic of trekking to the crown jewel of the park, Las Torres, in the early morning darkness to watch the sunrise hit them in the perfect light. Taking their advice to heart, after making camp, Jo and I cooked a quick dinner and jumped into the tent extremely early with alarms set for four a.m.

The cold was biting when we woke up that morning and the fog from our breath could be seen as an ominous haze in the light of our headlamps. Double layers of merino wool socks couldn't protect us from the cold fabric of our trail shoes until we at least started moving. I fired up the stove and quickly rehydrated a batch of chili for us. Thankfully we had our packs prepared the night before so as to spend as little stationary time in the morning cold as possible.

We started moving by 4:20 a.m., stumbling our way through the mucky and wet trail system. It seemed never-ending in the dark with only the small beam of light shining from our headlamps guiding us up a slippery muddy incline. Anytime we took a break I would look up into the darkness of the night. With hardly any light pollution and a perfectly clear sky, the stars were remarkable. Seeing the stars in these remote places was my absolute favorite because you can't reproduce it for anyone, largely because I am not talented enough to take a picture that comes even close to illustrating how incredible they were. I always felt the stars were like a personal keepsake for me and only me when exploring these remote places around the world.

A few hours later we started to encounter snow and ice as we scrambled up a scree field and the bright orange sun began to rise. The tall, magnificent towers that had painted the skyline for so many days were closer than they had ever been.

The wind was relentless now that we were unguarded by the trees so we found a large boulder with a crescent-shaped opening to sit under for protection. Ahead of us lay a glass-like lake in front of three magnificent towers of granite; Las Torres. They almost didn't look real; it was as if they had been sculpted from the Earth with a chisel by a wonderfully artistic giant.

Fifteen minutes went by and we still sat under the boulder snapping pictures and sipping from our frosty water bottles until the sun's light began to strike the tops of the towers. With only one other person at the base, we were experiencing something only three people could ever say they had on this day. First, a pink hue took over the sandy white-colored rock. Moments later, the towers were showered in a spectacular golden light that to this day is one of the most beautiful things I have ever seen. After only four minutes, the gold was gone and the towers appeared in the normal color of daylight. Four minutes, that was it. And we were fortunate enough to bear witness to it.

The hike down was completed with permanent smiles on our faces. What we had done in the pitch-dark was now revealed to us: spectacular views of the valley and drop-offs that would have turned our stomachs had we known they were there. We made it back down to our camp and packed up to hike on for one last night in Torres del Paine. Every minute I reveled in how lucky we were to have spent the past five days in one of the most extraordinary nooks of our beautiful world.

As we returned to Puerto Natales and checked back into Wild, the immense presence of the fifty-mile race, now only two days away, began to make itself known. Adding up the distances of the past five days of hiking, we realized that, although beautiful, we had traveled well over sixty miles in less than comfortable weather, an extra stress perhaps not welcomed by our bodies. Now we had to cover almost the same distance, but in one day.

My feet were throbbing like never before and I removed my socks to find a mangled mess of flesh. Tears, blisters, and mud adorned every aspect of both feet. And to the idea of the race ahead, I thought, *no fucking way*.

Jo and I went back to La Guanaca that night and our favorite waitress, Nadia, served us more delicious pizzas and our favorite, pisco sour. While trying to enjoy our first meal in civilization in days, the topic of the race distance dominated the dinner conversation.

"We can always drop down to the fifty-kilometer race. I really don't think I have fifty miles in me, Jo." I took a big swig from the glass of pisco in front of me.

"I know," she said with pain in her voice, "but let's not make a decision yet, we can think about it more tomorrow."

"Okay." I agreed. We were tired and weary, our judgment very clearly skewed by the protesting of our well-tested bodies. Tomorrow was our only real rest day of the trip, and it would be spent making the incredibly important decision of how much we wanted our bodies to suffer.

A lot was riding on this choice. If I decided to run the fifty-mile distance and not complete it, this would be my second unsuccessful South American marathon attempt and would not allow me to finish the continents in Asia later this year. If I dropped to the fifty-kilometer distance for the second time in only a few months, despite knowing I would complete the race I was sure I'd always regret it. These were all thoughts to be considered after a good night's rest in a clean dorm bed.

The next day I felt absolutely terrible. Almost everything hurt, but the worst was my feet. Never in my life had they been so damaged; stinging and throbbing from the abuse of the past week. In my head when I woke up, I knew what my stance would be on the inevitable distance debate with Jo today.

Contrary to what we had anticipated, it was almost painful to have a rest day with no expectation of activity. Knowing what was ahead, the impending physical monolith in front of us was mentally torturous. The temptation to drop nineteen miles of it was huge but thankfully, because of Jo, it didn't happen.

After hours and hours, swinging back and forth and making multiple pro/con lists, we stuck to the fifty-mile distance, pushed by Jo's incredible fortitude. I'll never forget that day, the two of us sitting in our hostel room, with pits in our stomachs. Eventually, we were committed, and it was time to get amped up. Tomorrow was going to be a massive undertaking, and we needed to start to prepare to be in the right mindset for it.

Downstairs at Wild, a comfortable living area decorated with paintings and sculptures from local artists created a super chilled-out vibe. Jari and Demaris were moving around the kitchen like dancers in a performance and a few guests sat quietly reading on the red cushioned benches. Light music capped off the relaxed tone, the whole place going a long way towards creating the Zen we badly needed.

"Tomorrow's the big day, Jari, fifty fucking miles!" I gave him a light punch on the shoulder as I said it.

"You crazy sons of bitches. You're going to do some kick-ass tomorrow! You want a little smoke? Always made me feel good before big day. Help you get into the zone, be mentally sharp," he said in his strong Finnish accent.

Jo and I laughed. "I think I'm good on that man, but I would love a beer."

Jari moved behind the counter and poured out a pint for me. "You know," he said, "when I was fighting Russians in the Finnish Army, we would have to go out in the forest for days at a time. Just skiing, skiing, skiing, hundreds of kilometers. It was so fucking cold. So cold and so much snow that you would have to dig holes in the snow to make an ass-cake in, but your mind would be so sharp and so fierce, and we got them every time! You guys will be strong like that tomorrow and win this competition for us, ya?"

"Not sure if we'll win man, but we'll sure try like hell to make you proud!" I finished my pint and we retreated upstairs to do our final prep, ready for the four a.m. wake-up call that I knew would come all too soon.

We diligently read the mandatory gear list to each other while we checked our packs, making sure everything was accounted for. Then I tended to my feet, performing minor surgery to repair the missing skin from my battered appendages, one section even requiring a combination of Moleskin and Dermabond to properly bandage my heel back together.

Everything was now prepared for us to run almost twenty miles further than we ever had in our entire lives tomorrow. Over the fifty miles we would gain over 10,000 feet including a full mountain to climb at mile twenty. If there was one thing I knew about tomorrow, success or failure, it was going to be an epic day.

Sleepless nights were common when working in healthcare, that I was used to, but the pre-race jitters that night paralleled those of my first marathon. In a twisted way, I loved it—pushing your distance further and further and doing things you weren't sure if you could complete or not were the ultimate drive for me in this sport. The thrill of the unknown tends to fuel the passion for adventure.

I felt as though I had only slept for an hour when my iPhone alarm signaled the start of the incredibly long day ahead. Jo and I sleepily grabbed our pre-packed bags and made for the bus pickup just a few hundred meters from Wild. Crazily enough, I was actually able to sleep for much of the bus ride to the start line. A nervous energy blanketed the inside of the bus, keeping everyone silent for the majority of the trip.

It was when we arrived at the gymnasium of the elementary school that would house the runners prior to heading to the start line that all the nervous chatter began. There were only eighty or so athletes in the fifty-miler, the first year this distance had been added to the event. Next year, we found out that they planned on appropriately shortening the name of the event to just "Ultra Paine."

The eighty of us coped with the pre-race stress in different ways. Some milled about nervously, others like Jo and I sat silently in an exercise of final mental preparedness, and a few South Americans laughed and smiled as they kicked a soccer ball back and forth to each other, undaunted by the coming hours.

We had one last check-in with race staff before we were ushered outside into the still dark and cold morning air. People jumped up and down to keep warm, swinging and stretching their legs in every which way. Jo and I gave each other one last hug for good luck and then the whistle sounded to commence our daylong adventure through the Patagonian wilderness.

Jo and I had decided to run this race together as a team. We wanted to be sure we finished the race and did not care about running a specific time. This way, we could keep each other in check and make sure neither of us was moving too quickly out of the gate. Double the supplies and safety in numbers, it was nice to have the company and added a much appreciated level of comfort to the already stressful day.

Fifteen miles flew by as fast as they could in terms of a hilly ultra marathon. It was the stunning beauty in every direction that distracted us from the pain. Cresting a hill we suddenly came to a steep drop-off that made me believe we had taken a wrong turn, but then I saw small dots almost one hundred meters below moving swiftly downwards. This was the course.

Black diamond ski trails in the United States were more gradual than the descent we were about to endure. Carefully and methodically, we switchbacked our way down, each step rapidly calculated in our brains so as not to twist an ankle. It was treacherous and absolutely insane. I was already nervous about the ascents; never had I thought I would be so concerned about a downhill.

At the bottom, we were greeted with an aid station to refill our bottles and were graciously offered a few pieces of chocolate that tasted better than a hamburger at a Fourth of July cookout. Even better was that the next three miles were on perfectly flat ground, running across wide-open fields that stretched on for miles.

The relief and enjoyment of the flat section was short-lived though, as we knew what awaited us ahead, an obstacle that had loomed in our minds since signing up for the race. It was the big and jagged bump in the elevation profile that Jo and I had stared at for so long every time we reviewed a course map. It was a 2,000-foot ascent over the span of just about one mile that was essentially climbing a mountain directly in the middle of the race.

It began at mile twenty, and it was impossible/stupid not to walk up it. We needed to grind it out, slow and steady if we wanted to get through this. The higher we got, the more we could see out over the valley. Other runners slowly moved up with us, higher and higher, and at one point I heard a few people gasp. Quickly, I turned in the direction of their stares to see what had taken their breath away.

As I looked out into the crystal clear sky, I saw a massive wingspan flying gracefully towards us: a condor. The giant bird flew just overhead and circled around a few times before flying away towards the mountains; just when I thought this race could not be any more beautiful.

When we finally reached the summit of the mountain that had instilled dread in us for so long, we were running on snow instead of rock. It felt good to be finally running instead of hiking, stretching our legs wildly and freely, bouncing across the ridgeline. My Garmin data showed that the total time for that mile was just over thirty-four minutes, not too bad, all thing considered. Now we were rewarded greatly with the privilege of running on top of a ridge with a 360-degree panoramic view of the mountains. We could see glaciers and turquoise lakes, beautiful fields, forest, and snowy mountains everywhere we looked. I now knew I had a new answer when someone asked me which part of the world I thought was the most beautiful and which race was my favorite.

Running across the top of this mountain typified why traveling to run had begun to heal me regardless of the turmoil I faced, be it the bombing or Rachel's death. Being in such immense beauty and feeling so small because of it was simply pure joy. I was also able to share it with one of my best friends. It reaffirmed all the decisions and sacrifices I had made to be here. I was mentally content and where I needed to be to get through the next thirty miles with Jo.

We descended down from the mountain back to level ground. With the largest climb in the rearview, it was now a game of energy conservation to get us to the finish line. The first water crossing was through a river so swift that a fixed rope was in place to prevent being swept away. The water was icy and pulled on our legs hungrily, but it was not to be outdone by an unplanned for crossing an hour later, just before mile forty.

Although it was not on the map, a rapid influx of rain had created a still water pond in the middle of the racecourse. The water here was well past my thighs and above Jo's waist. My mind began to think about the open cuts and wounds on my feet as I looked at the opaque brown color of the water we now waded through, surely full of foreign bacteria my body had never been exposed to before.

The high experienced earlier had been transient and I was fading fast, with only a few miles to go I was really starting to lose steam. My feet throbbed as the wounds sustained from the past week began to reopen and sting as dirt and sweat seeped into them. The intense aching in my quads was compounded by every step as the lactic acid continued to build, but worse than the physical pain was that my brain was beginning to give up. The dark nagging of that voice that tells you to *just stop* made the relatively tiny portion of the race left to us seem impossible.

My weapon was Jo, who kept morale high, urging us forward together, even when she probably had enough energy to finish ahead of me. We emerged from the bush and crossed the line together in sixteenth and seventeenth place with the most stunning backdrop of a race finish I could have ever dreamed of. I clicked "stop" on my Garmin, which now read, 12:27:54. That was a damn long time to be running, and I was very lucky to have had such an awesome friend and teammate to spend it with.

After a few photos we made it inside the hotel at the finish to get our drop bags. I pulled out the two PBRs stored in mine, and Jo cracked them open for us. The luxurious pasta dinner promised to us in the race flyer proved to be the South American equivalent of Ramen noodles, a devastating finding that was only slightly numbed by the taste of the Pabst.

Feeling accomplished, fulfilled, and beyond proud of ourselves, we made our way to the shuttle back to Puerto Natales. Of the eighty people who started the race only forty-four finished. I had completed the South American leg of my marathon challenge and Jo was the second woman to cross the finish line, an incredible achievement to celebrate on what was already a special day.

The bus left the finish line area of hotel Río Serrano and we were both asleep within minutes, only waking when the bus came to a stop back in Puerto Natales. Groggily, we grabbed our two bags and made the painful shuffle back to Wild, just before midnight.

I barely remember taking a shower, but I do recall the amount of skin that came off with my socks when I pulled them from my feet. The true sign of a hard-fought battle on an ass-kicking racecourse. Before my head hit the pillow I was asleep; proud, content, and completely beat.

I walked downstairs the next morning with Jo and we were received with massive hugs from Jari, Demaris, Isa, and Josh. Over our time at Wild we grew incredibly close to them. Jo proudly got to tell Jari that she won her category and was the second overall woman, and he beamed with excitement. It felt completely natural when Jari proceeded to extend a job offer to me; the chance to stay and explore this spectacular corner of the world whilst working in a place I truly felt at home. I painfully declined his offer, relaying what felt like my inevitable answer and yet not quite sure why it had to be so.

When the time came to leave, I gave Jari one of my paramedic patches and explained to him how when I met people I felt I really connected to, I would give them one as a memento of friendship. He put it in a special place behind the counter on a shelf next to a vase. When he did so, he also removed a small leather-bound book.

"This is our secret book," he said as he opened the cover. "Obviously, we like all our guests, but some are more special than others." With that, he winked. "To those guests, we ask you to write your contact info and address, so when we shut down for winter, maybe we come visit. If you like, we would love for you to be in our book."

WILD

We felt incredibly privileged and excited to be included in this book full of other travelers from all corners of the world. We truly hoped that they would reach out to come visit us one day.

Demaris called us a taxi and it was one I wished would never come.

Nonetheless, we shouldered our bags and one more exchange of big hugs filled the entryway before we left. After a ten-minute ride and then a three-hour bus to Punta Arenas, we were on a plane heading home to the United States.

Why didn't I just stay in Puerto Natales, working at Wild for the unforeseeable future?

As liberated as I feel on these adventures, there is still some sort of structure that I desire as if to not feel totally detached from my "normal" upbringing in the United States. By no means was I following the all too common expectation in the U.S. of high school, college, full-time job, get married, have kids, work until sixty-five, and call it a life. There is no way I could do that, I simply would not be happy. I was brought up to believe that what we have in the United States, this cookie-cutter lifestyle, is the right thing to do and deviation is rebelling. I know I'm judged for not following "normalcy" and the conventional path by friends and even some family. With as much as I deviate from that standard, it seems I still crave some of it. I wonder often if I'll always be on the move with no real stability. But what's wrong with that? There are all kinds of normal and I hope that everyone who doesn't fit that mold realizes that. I didn't feel weird or wrong for not fitting myself into what society likes to think is best for me. I was being honest and true to myself, following those diversions and dreams, which too often stay as just that. In some ways this connection with and real honoring of our desires could be viewed as the true pinnacle of happiness.

I imagine that my decisions and my lifestyle were hard to understand for those without the knowledge of what had driven them. My real reason for the seemingly rash path I had taken, that a terrorist attack and the death of a close friend still haunted me, was something I shared with very few. Sure it was hard when people criticized me and my choices, or they questioned my parents for not reigning me in on my "renegade millennial selfishness," but I had to let it go. My parents are truly amazing, and I am beyond lucky that they support my hopes and dreams because I know it's difficult for them too. Cutting through the external voices and expectations, I could still hold on to the core truth of this mission. The truth being that with each day I spent in the wilderness or in far off lands, my mind and soul were healing. The wonderful adventure of running a marathon on all seven continents was accomplishing exactly what it was supposed to. This wildly amazing plan was working.

I continued to learn to embrace the mountains as a way of feeling close to Rachel, instead of fearing them as a place that would rekindle painful memories. It became something to look forward to, hiking into the mountains, even the ones most familiar to me, so that I could talk and connect with her again. Now, after realizing the damage that had been caused by suppressing my feelings from the Boston Marathon bombing, I was attempting to handle this in a healthier manner. Most importantly, I recognized that it was okay to not be okay, and did not feel the same anger and shame that had only compounded my pain following the bombing. Some days were good, some not so much, but as time passed I made sure that every day resulted in some sort of progress.

Just a single continent was left on the list now. In this insane and epic journey that had taken me all around the globe, only one corner remained untouched. I needed to prepare myself for the biggest and highest race of my life in the heart of Asia.

CHAPTER NINE

TOP OF THE WORLD

Namche Bazaar, Nepal
November 2017

My choice for a race in Asia required days of searching through a tantalizing spread of events, most with websites lacking any sort of English translation. The big ones that people suggested were the well-known Great Wall Marathon and Petra Desert Marathon, but those did not quite fit the small trail race feel that I was seeking. Getting this one right was important; it was the last time I would ever have to make a decision on a piece of my seven continents journey. A strange feeling of detached disbelief came over me whenever I remembered that I was actually starting to plan my final race.

I was comfortably set up with my laptop in the corner of a small café with multiple web browsers open when a Google search brought me across an event that I must have overlooked in my prior research. I stumbled across the Everest Marathon, a race that was recognized by the Guinness Book of World Records as the "highest marathon in the world." It required an extensive application process to gain entry to the high altitude race, which was prepared by an organization operating out of the U.K. If you were selected, weeks of trekking in the Himalaya were mandated to acclimatize and get up to the start line; a start line that sat above the clouds at just shy of 17,000 feet. The race route followed the traditional path to Everest Base Camp with the start of the race located just slightly lower at Gorak Shep, in the shadow of Mount Everest. In the past, I had never had much of a desire to travel to Nepal, but after that fortuitous discovery as I sipped a sugary coffee, it swiftly moved to the top of the list.

The race was one year away when I first discovered it, and the application cycle had fittingly opened a few days prior. Because it was a relatively small field, they made sure to note that spots generally filled rather quickly. Hastily, I completed the application that same day, attached my running resume, and fired it off with my fingers crossed.

A few weeks later I was accepted into the 2017 race. I finally knew that with enough preparation, the journey to complete a marathon on all seven continents would conclude in November. Never had I imagined what it would feel like to have the finite ending in sight. The finish line to the continents had never seemed tangible until this very moment and it was a peculiar feeling indeed, bittersweet in many ways.

Amongst the many forms and documents required to be filled out and returned to the race company was a medical waiver to be completed by a doctor. Unlike Patagonia, I did not forge any signatures; I obeyed instructions and actually had my primary care physician fill it out properly. When explaining the race to him, he shook his head and laughed without making any attempt to discourage me. He knew any attempts to change my mind would be futile and I felt fortunate to have a physician that might not accept, but at least tolerated my adventures.

On the East Coast of the United States, it's nearly impossible to train at altitude. Our highest peak in New England is Mount Washington, standing at 6,288 feet above sea level and infamous for having some of the worst weather in the world. The start line of the Everest Marathon was located at almost three times this height, a staggering 16,942 feet. The only way to prepare was to build up my endurance and treat this regular distance marathon as if it were something like a fifty-miler. The months flew by as the intensity of my training increased with each page of the calendar.

Autumn brought the challenge of scattering Rachel's ashes on the summit of her favorite peak in the White Mountains, Mount Garfield. On a crisp September day, a group of us, including her mother, carried her to the top so she could enjoy the mountain she had loved so much for the rest of time. My mind raced on the way to the summit, memories flashing wildly across my brain as tears intermittently ran over my sweaty cheeks.

I distinctly remember the salt burning my eyes, flaring the anger that began to boil in my chest. This time, it wasn't anger directed toward Rachel, it was a fury at the world that she was gone, and that I would never walk with her on this trail or any other. I hope that one day these memories and places will be nostalgic and beautiful, but at that moment they only manifested as anger.

On top of the summit it was misty, only allowing quick peaks of hazy views over the Pemigewasset Wilderness. I thought of how many times Rachel had gazed out upon the vastness of trees and pointed granite peaks that were now obscured from our view, but I knew they were there, and I knew Rachel was too. On this day, like so many others, I tortured myself with the question that will never be answered, I wondered why she wanted to leave it all.

On a day that should have been full of beauty and remembrance, the emotion implanted in my memory was anger; anger that she'll never know how much I cared, and anger that I'll never truly know what she was facing. The only way I could think of to show her how much she mattered to me was to continue to show her the world she had left behind through my eyes.

With this motivation always close, and training taking up much of my time outside of work, it wasn't long before I found myself with my kit bag packed, ready to run a marathon on my seventh continent.

• • •

The smoggy thickness of the air that is a feature of every travel book on Nepal is a severe understatement. As soon as I stepped off the plane from Kuala Lumpur at ten p.m., I felt my lungs strain painfully against the abysmal air quality emanating from the teeming capital of pollution that is Kathmandu. Rushing into the airport, I stood in line for over an hour to obtain my visa. Then after retrieving my luggage, I exited the main terminal into a sea of chaos where the sharks were soliciting taxi drivers. Thankfully, I found the driver the race organizer had arranged for me fairly quickly and I gratefully hopped into the passenger seat.

Utterly exhausted, I arrived at the race headquarters hotel fifteen minutes later and was greeted by a large blue, "Welcome Everest Marathon Runners" banner in the front entry. The British race organizer, Diana, a woman in her seventies, briefly greeted me in the entryway and assisted me in getting checked in. It was starting to become real how near the conclusion of my journey was. After a long day of travel, I made it to a heavenly comfortable bed and drifted to sleep almost instantly.

The following morning was a whirlwind of checking kit bags and meeting countless people whose names I would have to commit to memory as we hiked the next three weeks to the start line of our race together. Aside from a twenty-two-year-old Scottish girl, I was the youngest on the trip, and in my group I was the only American. This naturally led to a barrage of jokes and chiding, as I assumed my natural role as the lone Yank in a room full of Brits.

I was assigned to the yellow team, which consisted of twenty runners and our group leader, Sally Ward, one of the kindest people I would meet in my time in Nepal. As I got to meet each of my team members from all over the world, I immediately was drawn to four Irishmen who had traveled over together from Dublin. I didn't know it as we exchanged background stories and forgot each other's names, but Frank Farrell, John Kelly, Daithi O'Murchu, and Tom Power would end up becoming lifelong friends of mine. Their incessant, warm banter and almost as incessant drinking defining our friendship.

We had two days of preparation in Kathmandu to stock up on any extra supplies we would need before flying to Lukla, where we would commence our long hike to the start line. As soon as we made it into the Himalaya the price of everything would increase in direct proportion to the altitude. So the Irish and myself ventured downtown to check out the local wool products, random hiking gear, and lastly to the grocery store to stockpile chocolate bars.

The streets of Kathmandu were crowded, polluted, and smelly. A smog blanket covered the air and it was impossible to be outside for more than five minutes without your throat being coated in an awful dust. My distaste for Kathmandu grew strong and fast as each blow of my nose revealed a new glob of black snot in the tissue.

We had to be careful of what we returned with for extra provisions, for our baggage restrictions were tight and Diana required us to have our luggage weighed before we could continue on to the airport. Kit bags had to be ten kilograms or less, and personal backpacks five kilograms or less. The restrictions were due to the exceptionally delicate nature of the flight into Lukla, the airport in the Himalaya where all Everest flights enter through. It wasn't until I experienced the plane ride that I understood what they meant by "delicate."

The morning of our flight was a blur. Alarm clocks buzzed prior to five a.m. and we were already on the hazy streets of Kathmandu before the sun was up. Sleepily waiting in the crammed domestic airport terminal for a few hours, the excitement dulled. When our flight number was finally called, in a chaotic, disorganized rush, we scrambled to the entry gate in stampede-like fashion.

Our group clambered into the side door of a tiny plane that sat no more than twenty people and within minutes we were flying out of the polluted city air and into mountains of size and beauty beyond wonder.

The mountains were so tall on the flight to Lukla that they could be seen in amazing clarity and detail as we passed over and in some cases, next to them. Lukla has an infamous reputation for being the most dangerous airport in the world. Runways generally aren't built into cliff edges, right? Excited smiles with more than a hint of relief were exchanged as our tiny craft eventually transitioned to a juddering trundle along the exposed tarmac. The take-off back to Kathmandu is even sketchier than this precarious landing challenge, requiring the plane to travel downhill on the runway and sometimes dropping off the edge like an aircraft carrier before regaining altitude.

After a short three-hour trek from the airport, our first night was a real trial run of being at altitude. We began a nighttime routine of eating very simple foods for dinner as to not distress the GI tract, (which would naturally be temperamental over the coming weeks) then retiring to bed very early. This first night also saw the initiation of a ritual of card games, which would become the most common activity to pass the hours of free time over the duration of our hike.

The next day was the first true test of endurance as we were slated to hike to the famed village of Namche Bazaar, the last major establishment before Everest. I allowed myself to enjoy the majority of this section on my own, appreciating the stark green trees contrasting with the blue sky and white-capped mountains. I felt the spike of energy running through my veins when I crossed over the rope suspension bridges strung high over the rivers. The cherry on top was getting my first glimpse of Mount Everest. Truly indescribable in both size and beauty, its majesty humbled me beyond anything I have experienced since.

It was a surreal experience to walk in to Namche Bazaar, the bustling cobblestone streets filled with crowded shops exactly how Jon Krakauer described it in *Into Thin Air*. I carefully walked up the steep steps of the main street, past bakeries, gear outfitters, cafes, and even the world's highest Irish pub.

It wasn't long until the others arrived and I rejoined my Irish gang along with the sixth member of our motley gang, Fiona Smith. Fiona was a reindeer herder from Scotland (I also did a double take) who would grow to be one of my closest friends long after our time in Nepal. We found a great spot for lunch and chowed down on veggie C-momos, a local specialty and a quick favorite of our group. We had an unneeded rest day tomorrow, so the plan was to resupply as this was the last proper place to do so for the next two weeks, rest, and then hit the Irish pub for our final big night out until after the marathon.

My day was spent wandering the streets in awe, thinking of all the famous climbers that have walked these same stones on their way to summit Everest. My friend, mentor, and coworker Jim Gagne had been here in 2006 prior to him becoming the first person born in New Hampshire to scale the famous peak.

I kept poking my head into different places and found a small shop with a little old Nepalese lady inside sitting on a dusty wooden chair. She smiled, stood up, and approached me as I walked through the entry. The tiny little building was full of all kinds of yak wool goods and she repeated the word "warm" multiple times as she handed me the different colored blankets. The material was so soft and the colors vibrant and beautiful. A bright blue blanket with purple and yellow stripes caught my eye and I had a hard time saying no, especially at the price of 1,000 Nepalese Rupee, or ten U.S. dollars.

Regrouping with the Irish briefly in the lodge, we set out in search of pizza before heading off to the pub. Pizza was a delicacy I would have never imagined enjoying at over 11,000 feet of altitude, nestled in the harsh climate of the Himalaya.

After finishing dinner we walked through the doors of the Irish pub for the first time, where the party in Namche was each and every night. A small place on the corner of the main street, it was adorned with broken couches, a slanted pool table, and flags and posters on the walls from all over the world. Memories of successful expeditions and good times had plastered every corner of space in the dimly lit barroom. The barman, Chris, was from Kathmandu but quite literally lived in the bar for the entire climbing season.

Beers and whiskeys were not counted and clocks were unheeded. The next morning I attended breakfast with a pounding head unrelated to the altitude, and a very small appetite. Slowly, I made my way down the streets, a haziness blanketing my delicate head.

The small shops that lined the alleyways had been depleted by our group of runners, and after only three days of hiking with the group, I began to notice how underprepared or inexperienced some of them were. Many gave off the impression that they had little to no backcountry or camping experience. Their attitude toward the supplies they carried and their expectations of the resources available were more lavish than I would have thought. Additionally, the race organization itself was now revealing itself to be somewhat disordered and lackadaisical for a dangerous and logistically complex event. This was Diana's last year being in charge of the event and the responsibilities were being passed on to another British woman with a fair bit less experience. This new woman had, thus far, come across very aloof and disorganized, seemingly lacking the demeanor necessary to be a race director. Diana was abrasive at baseline, but that's why she was good at being a race director. Her replacement's passiveness and inability to handle confrontation were a disastrous combination when leading a group of athletes; unfortunately renowned to be arrogant and egotistical.

Frank and I became vocal at a nightly meeting when a new bit of information was delivered to us, that we were "forbidden" to actually trek up to Everest basecamp, which was an astounding and previously unmentioned "law" now enforced by the race organizers. It was made clear that we would be disqualified from the race if it were to be found out that we ventured to Everest Base Camp on our own accord for "safety reasons." The Irish and myself were infuriated by the thought of this and very openly contested the "unwritten rule." There was absolutely no way we were going to be within a three-hour walk of base camp from Gorak Shep (the race start) and not make the extra effort to trek onto such a famed spot. This would be a battle we would continue to fight almost each day of the hike at our nightly group meetings.

All the real hiking began when we left Namche Bazaar. I initially spent most of my time with the four Irish guys, later finding myself at a similar pace with Fiona, with whom I spent nearly all of our walking time. Daithi and I spent a fair bit of time chatting about the incredible ultra distance races he had done around the world. He referred to himself as a shaman and had an incredibly spiritual outlook on life. When trekking together I found myself constantly joining him in giving thanks to mother universe and father sky for the blessing of being in the beauty of the Himalaya at this moment in time.

Some of the events he had competed in were just downright ridiculous. Multi-day stage races in the Yukon, South America, and anywhere else on the globe you could think of. Many of his stories involved near death to himself or others, so I had to ask the million dollar question, the one that I hated so much getting asked myself: why?

Everyone back home thinks that I'm insane when they hear about my plans and aspirations, but once you enter this circle, there's always someone crazier than you are.

The "why" question is generally never answered entirely or truthfully, largely because it is an incredibly complex explanation that has culminated from an entire lifetime of circumstances. But sometimes the "how" is answered.

"When you were literally frozen, and were close to death, how'd you do it, Daithi? What the hell pulled you through that?" By the time he had finished telling me about some of his experiences, especially in arctic racing, I would find myself mouth agape and mind spinning a million miles per hour.

"Well, you see," his Irish brogue thick but moving quickly in an excited tone, "you have one happy thought. And you cling to it, and you hold onto it, and you save it for when you need it most." He paused. "But you must know it completely and be able to draw from it effortlessly and visualize it perfectly. If you find yourself in a dark place with the light fading, you bring that to the front of your mind. Let it carry you through when you can no longer carry yourself."

I took this piece of advice and thought long about it, then tucked it away for later.

We continued on, deviating from the Everest Base Camp route to the west as part of our acclimatization plan. We would ascend to higher altitude, remaining there for a few days, then return back down the route to Gorak Shep before going up again.

The air was incredibly dry, which was further compounded by the constant flow of dust particles in the air that the yaks kicked up on their daily trudges. Soon everyone, including myself, had developed the rather annoying "Everest cough" that can persist for three to six weeks even after leaving the Himalaya. The hacking noise of expelling dust from a dry throat surprisingly becomes like white noise after only a few days.

Sneezing also plagued me, the dirt turning the snot into a disgusting brown-tinged mucus. Toilet paper was like gold up here so it was also rather frustrating to have to use it on something other than your bottom.

We spent a few days in Machermo, hovering around 14,670 feet in altitude. Much of the free time was spent playing an unimaginable amount of card games, as we often finished hiking just after midday. Since safely acclimatizing to be able to run a marathon at altitude was the priority, the days were often very short.

Machermo allowed for much needed rest, letting muscles heal for our only opportunity to bag a peak in the Himalaya during our acclimatization. We set out for the town of Gokyo close to six a.m. with hopes to scale to the summit of Gokyo Ri around noontime, some 17,575 feet above sea level.

When I arrived in town I waited for the others and signed my permit form to summit the peak. The first to arrive were Fiona, an Englishman named Chris, and the young Scot, Shauney.

Briefly pausing for a rest, we continued on together up the mountain at a brisk pace, standing atop the summit much earlier than noon. Unlike Kilimanjaro, the temperature was not sub-zero at this altitude, allowing ample time for photos and to enjoy the majestic view of Everest on a crystal-clear day. The unusually calm weather and the protection of our thick down jackets allowing us to be almost comfortable just under 18,000 feet.

Anytime I was on a high peak, I still always thought of Rachel. Depending on what you view as the physical location of heaven, or if you view it as an actual tangible place, I always believed that the higher I was, the closer I was to Rach. She would have treasured this, like the White Mountains of New Hampshire that she loved so much, only much, much bigger. I'll still always wonder why she did it, and I'll never know why. I think about her every day, and especially in circumstances where I am awestruck by the enormity and beauty of the world. How I wished she could be here to see and feel the incredible power of the highest place on our planet. I continued to wonder if a day would go by soon where she was not on my mind; writing this now I wonder the same question, and have to accept that perhaps I am still not finished processing her death.

Just as I had promised her on Kilimanjaro, I hoped that she was now able to take in the magnificence of the landscape set before me through my own eyes. Turquoise glacial lakes dotted the valleys far below and the 8,000-meter peaks strewn in all directions were the mightiest of backdrops. Gusts of wind high above were blowing snow from the pinnacles of their jagged peaks, creating cloud-like apparitions in the bluebird sky. *Well, I hope you're enjoying this as much as I am Rach,* I thought silently to myself.

We returned to camp that night feeling that beautiful mixture of accomplishment and exhaustion. Additionally, blowing up a Therm-a-Rest sleeping pad while at altitude doesn't do too much to liven you up. I passed out in my tent almost instantly, dreaming of tomorrow's day off.

Only the rest day never happened. Fiona and I woke up feeling rather excellent given the circumstances of sleeping at altitude and having scaled a peak over 5,000 meters the day before. The thought of being stagnant at camp all day was mentally devastating to both of us whilst we were surrounded by such an amazing landscape and trail system. We were then struck with a rather ambitious idea—to gather an order from everyone in our group, and take a walk back to Gokyo, to the world's highest bakery.

Within an hour of waking up, accompanied by our fearless leader Sally, we began the ten-mile round-trip hike back to Gokyo for the second day in a row. Our packs were empty and ready to be filled with cakes and pastries. We had surveyed the group at breakfast and collected an order of six brownies, two donuts, two chocolate croissants, two cinnamon rolls, and a slice of apple pie, plus the two packs of cookies that we would pick up for the Sherpas as a token of appreciation.

When we arrived in Gokyo, the baker was ecstatic with the order we placed, clearing out the majority of the pastries he had made for the day. Tea and pie for us was ordered as well and we sat down to enjoy our rewards before returning back to Machermo for lunch.

Walking back was otherworldly. The three of us walked as fast or slow as we chose amongst open plains on a blue-sky day with temperatures warm enough to strip down into a light base layer. Running through those wide-open fields sheltered by the high peaks of the Himalaya was one of the more magical experiences I've had in my travels and definitely my favorite day in Nepal.

Thanksgiving was a few days later, and for the first time since beginning to travel the world, I felt the physical pangs of homesickness. I had been eating camp food for two weeks (and for stomach safety had been entirely vegetarian) and couldn't help but envision my family gathered around the table with a nice roast turkey, all the fixings, and my mom's homemade brownies for dessert. I described the meal in detail to Daithi as we descended the valley down into the remote village of Pheriche.

The intensity of experience and the openness between myself, the Irish, and Fiona allowed us to create an incredible bond, becoming very in-tune to each other's emotions over only a short period of time. They could tell that today was a bit more difficult for me. So once camp was set up and gear dumped in our tents, we set off in search of the town bakery. It was a fruitful trip, the owner even making each of us a tiny personal apple pie to celebrate the American holiday, but that wasn't all. That night at our group meeting, once everything was finished, Tom came over to me with a portable speaker playing Bruce Springsteen's "Born in the U.S.A." He then proceeded to hand me a gallon-sized Ziploc bag full of goods including a candy bar, Clif Bar, beef jerky, pieces of toilet paper, a Thanksgiving card, and a can of beer that we split amongst six of us.

My incredibly amazing Everest group had put together a Thanksgiving package for their lone American in the middle of the Himalaya.

The day after Thanksgiving we continued to Lobuche, and the select group of us that defied executive orders went on a "hush-hush" trip up to Everest Base Camp.

If it weren't for the novelty and legend of this place, the trip outside of climbing season is just to see a baron glacier. Being the Everest nerd I am, I was still enthralled by the history of where we stood, the view of the icefalls, and the tantalizing sight of the pathway that leads to the roof of the world. When we arrived at the marker signifying Everest Base Camp, I opened my pack to remove my Tom Brady jersey for a photograph. Then something amazing happened. John pointed to the center of the marker, and said, "Bobby! Isn't that your man's jersey right there?"

I turned around and to my surprise, amongst the array of country flags, sign memorials, and rocks engraved with achievements, lay a Tom

Brady jersey, in the middle and most prominent position of all. In that moment, it was reaffirmed for me that TB12 is indeed the greatest human to ever walk the face of this planet.

We returned to the camp with the vigor and energy of little kids who knew they had fought the authority and won. Ready to face an onslaught of verbal attacks and threats to our race qualification, our arguments were prepared and ready, but we received no pushback. No one spoke of it or questioned what we had done. It was that simple and I was beyond shocked, but I was not complaining. Feeling accomplished and content, we continued upwards again, now only two sleeps away from race day.

The weeks of acclimatizing and hiking to the start had worn the group down, and the night before the race at Gorak Shep (16,942 feet) it was really beginning to show. Something similar to norovirus was running rampant through camp inducing spells of vomiting and diarrhea amongst almost all of my team. On top of the GI distress, altitude sickness amplified the symptoms that many of the athletes were suffering from. Regarding Gorak Shep, Wikipedia states, "At this altitude, few people feel comfortable and many start to suffer the symptoms of altitude sickness or acute mountain sickness."

Fortunately, I was one of the very few that remained healthy. Conversely to what you might imagine, being healthy induced a state of paranoia in me, anxious of what could happen on one of the most important "marathon eves" of my running career.

Isolating myself from the group, I went off to bed early in a self-implemented quarantine state. It was too cold and I was too nervous to even think about the fact that tomorrow would hopefully mark the end of my seven continents marathon journey. Drifting off, bundled tightly in the yak wool blanket that lined my sleeping bag, my only thoughts revolved around keeping all my fluids inside of me. I did not want to suffer the fate of some of my poor friends that had already decided to not even toe the start line in the morning.

The alarm clock was supposed to ring just before five a.m., but my biological clock beat it, just as it did in Boston so many years ago. That seemed so long ago now. Never could I have imagined, as that nineteen year old at the start of the 2013 Boston Marathon the horror that lay ahead of me or the journey that would arise as a consequence of that day. That only four years later, I would wake up shivering in a sleeping bag preparing to begin the highest marathon in the world in the heart of the Himalaya.

Hardworking Sherpas were my only company for the first few minutes of breakfast, consisting of none other than porridge and tea. Visualizing the mush sloshing around my stomach for the next 26.2 miles instantly deterred any notion of attempting to finish the porridge.

As others began to join me, I pulled out the Clif Bar that Daithi had contributed to my yellow team Thanksgiving package. The usual crew of John, Tom, Frank, and Fiona sat down around me as I peeled back the all too familiar packaging.

Nervous tension was obviously felt by everyone, silencing even Tom from his normal comedic act. He and Frank had both fallen ill during the night. Tom awoke to Frank literally throwing up into his trekking boots, which triggered his own bout of sickness. As I looked around me, it appeared that no one was ready for the Everest Marathon.

Still feeling physically okay, but internally a mental wreck, I made one last trip to the bathroom before we got the call to head out to the start line.

This was it, I thought to myself, checking my kit one last time. It was fairly empty because I was already wearing most of the mandatory layers on my body. Even with the down jacket pulled tightly over me, the cold rattled my bones as soon as the biting wind smacked against my face. The temperature on race morning: negative four degrees Fahrenheit.

We counted off our bib numbers in a role call manner to ensure everyone was at the start line. I was barely paying attention to the voices around me when I realized it was my turn to yell "Twenty!" My head swirled in a million different directions, strategizing my approach to the day. As soon as the race started I would ditch my large down jacket, to be returned in Namche Bazaar, even though the cold would quickly set in. So my plan was to take off at a quick enough pace to warm my muscles, but not so fast that the altitude would strike me down over the first few miles. The next few hours would be a delicate balance of toying with my physiology. The more I thought about it, the more I wished I had chosen a simpler race for Asia.

My thoughts were interrupted by the race official shouting, "Go!" The sixteen Nepalese runners took off as if it were your local charity five-kilometer race. The screwed up thing was that I tried to take off with them. I had rehearsed this so many times in my head, namely how I would *not* do that, but I was so cold, and just needed to move as quickly as I could. Just over one hundred meters into the race we encountered the first incline where I caught up with some of the Nepalese women. I realized I was in trouble as my lungs screamed from the effort of climbing, and I probably looked like an idiot for being up there with them. As we crested the hill, I was nearly out of breath and adjusted my pace into a more comfortable stride for the altitude, allowing me to settle in with the front of the Western runners.

For the first half of the marathon, everything could not have been more perfect. We passed back through Lobuche, the checkpoint in Dughla, and then past Pheriche where I had celebrated Thanksgiving just a few days before. Continuing past Debuche, the temperature had warmed up enough for me to drop my top layer and ditch my tights and thermals for running shorts.

In fact I was wearing the same running shorts that I had worn during my first-ever road race in Falmouth over six years ago. Everything was coming full circle and for whatever stupid reason, the clothes I would wear in my finish line picture mattered to me more than they ever had. I had envisioned what it would be like crossing that line for so long, the crowning achievement on a journey spanning years that had taken me around the entire globe. My head would be tossed back with hands held high holding up seven fingers. That's the way it happened in every dream I had ever had about this moment, and now it was only thirteen miles away.

For the past several miles I had the pleasure of running with Fiona over the beautiful mountainsides. The company was welcome and by running together we held each other accountable for not moving too quickly, while also pushing each other enough to keep it interesting.

We both made it to the mile fourteen checkpoint in Tengboche where one of the expedition doctors was serving rice pudding and evaluating our mid-race condition. Still feeling great, I tried rice pudding for the first time in my life, and it was awful. We chatted back and forth about the difficulty of the course thus far and we informed her about the sickness that plagued the camp last night. Although it was a net downhill, due to the mountainous terrain, there was a gain close to 10,000 feet over the distance of the race. One of the major contributors to this total was a hill just after our current position. Fiona left before me while I procrastinated by stomaching down another gel to extinguish the vile rice pudding taste from my mouth.

Not wanting to delay any further, I set off down a steep incline knowing that soon enough I would gain most of it back. The descent flew by. Galloping over rocks and skidding on loose dirt, I made it to the bottom with both ankles fully intact.

The trudge uphill was slow and cumbersome. I was slogging through in a regular rhythm when it suddenly hit—that dreaded first pang of nausea. It was a warning sign, signaling the inevitable was coming no matter how much I fought to deny it.

A few minutes later I was spewing rice pudding over the side of a cliff. Wiping my beard, I slugged back some water and continued on. But then again, I vomited. And again, and again.

The vicious attack only lasted two minutes, during which I vowed that this was the first and last time I would ever eat rice pudding. Drinking a bit more water flavored with my favorite pineapple electrolyte mix, my legs carried me further up the hill.

However, the nausea did not dissipate and shortly after I resumed moving, I stopped again on the side of the trail to puke. Then the diarrhea came. The reality began to hit, that the rice pudding wasn't the villain. Whatever virus was plaguing the camp last night simply decided to strike me later than it had the others. My heart sunk. I didn't know if I would be able to finish the race.

There was no bathroom to run into, no couch to curl up on, and no one to comfort me, I was alone and felt absolutely terrible. There was only one way to move—forward. Putting one foot in front of the other, slowly at first, but then picking up into a trot, I attempted to get back on track.

The jostling of my stomach induced another round of vomiting. Hands on my knees, I doubled over, staring down at the now-tainted trail. *I'll walk for a bit*, I thought to myself. *That'll give it some time to clear.* But it didn't, not even a little bit. No longer was I able to intake any water, gel, or food without my body immediately rejecting it. My stomach groaned and my head pounded from the new onslaught of physiological turmoil in my body.

The severity of the situation sank in. This wasn't a normal race where eleven to twelve miles left meant an hour and a half back to beers with the guys. It would be a three-hour minimum before catching a glimpse of the finish line. The temperature was now dropping as I generated less body heat with my slowed pace, and the altitude was fighting against me in every possible way. Pushing the "worst-case scenario" thoughts out of my head, I continued onward.

In the area of mile eighteen, I came along a dramatic cliff edge where I observed the most magnificent view of Mount Everest I had seen yet. There it was, in all its glory, the highest point on our humble little planet. My legs stopped moving, I paused and stared, awestruck by the mountain. A wisp of snow hung idle in the air, recently swept off the summit by lofty winds. Clouds began to obscure the foreground and

I observed a shadow creep over the face of the high peak. The newly overcast sky returned a chill to the air that reminded me to re-layer since I had been walking for much of the past few miles.

Pondering this, I turned away from Everest and continued down the trail, but oddly, the shadow of the mountain did not disappear from my field of view. I blinked my eyes but the shadow remained. This was how I first realized I was losing my vision. I could not see anything out of the corner of my right eye; additionally, a small amount of my left field of view also abandoned me.

Navigating myself along a windy cliff path was the last place I wanted to be whilst fighting to maintain the ability to see. This is truly when the panic set in. The mantra in my mind was to keep moving forward, but it became increasingly difficult as my sight lessened while I continued to move on.

By mile nineteen, I had lost almost all my vision in the right eye and it felt like I was looking through a pinhole out of my left. It wasn't safe for me to be moving at this point so I sat myself down on a rock. It was cold against my ass in an almost soothing way. My body could feel the dehydration and sense the nearing state of hypoglycemia. Having vomited everything up and been consistently nauseous for over an hour, I desperately needed to get something in my stomach. Caloric intake needed to be greatly increased while at this altitude in normal circumstances, let alone two thirds of the way through a marathon with a stomach bug.

I took small sips from my water bottle and puked almost instantly. Soon I would be running out of anything at all to throw back up. From my endless time studying the course, I knew there was a checkpoint at mile twenty, and that became the new goal, I just had to get there.

My tunnel vision had improved slightly, allowing me to leave the comfort of the rock and make my way towards my new beacon, which stood on a hill overlooking Namche Bazaar. After a few steps forward, I felt as decent as I could and began to make my way down a set of stairs.

Seconds later, I found myself tumbling down those same stairs, my impaired vision causing me to miss a hole in the stone steps.

My luck, I thought, and quickly put myself back on my feet before inspecting the extent of my injuries. Very sore, but nothing serious, my tired legs continued to carry my failing body.

The mile twenty checkpoint was like a lighthouse in the dangerous sea that this race had become for me. A Scottish doctor began to evaluate me and asked how I was doing. "Great!" I attempted to say with a burst of enthusiasm, but only vocalized it as a slight whimper.

"Well, that's a lie if I ever heard one!" He retorted with an extremely thick accent.

The mile twenty checkpoint brought the race all the way back to Namche Bazaar, the same town as the finish line. Runners would then, however, embark on the Thamo Loop, a 6.2-mile stretch that would make the race a full distance marathon. Runners too exhausted had the option to forego the Thamo Loop, earning themselves a certificate, but no medal, no marathon finish, and in my case, no completion of the seven continents. The decision was simple. While the doctor was turned away distracted by speaking to a colleague, I sprung up and ran off towards the Thamo Loop, forgoing his approval to continue.

My brain was having an internal argument with my gut. Upstairs, my mind was fixated on finishing the continents at any cost. It had been almost three weeks of hiking to get to this point, but it had been almost four years of hard work that brought me to this moment. And now, only ten kilometers away from the most important goal in my life, there was no way I was stopping. A deep and visceral instinct inside me knew this was the wrong decision.

Passing mile twenty-one, a bizarre sensation flooded through my body, something I had never felt before. Every part of me felt sick and weak. Although some of my vision had returned it was no longer the same, and oftentimes it was distorted.

I was so ill that I was now beginning to hallucinate. Colors danced across my field of view, the bushes frequently moved places they shouldn't, and the path wiggled in unnatural ways. It had been almost three hours since my last drink of fluid or consumption of any type of food. I was dehydrated, presumably hypoglycemic, hypothermic, and the excruciating pain in my flank and lower back felt like my kidneys were beginning to shut down. On top of these issues, the altitude was taking full advantage of my weakened state.

I staggered along the trail, desperate to make it to the end point at mile twenty-three where a Sherpa would tie a ribbon around my running pack, proving I had made it to the end point of the Thamo Loop. Among the myriad of deranged thoughts, I struggled to stay motivated, my goal becoming less tangible with every minute I spent in this altered mind state.

Upon making it to the top of a rock-strewn hill, I suddenly had the overwhelming urge to shit. For whatever reason, my severely impaired brain now decided that above everything else, this now took precedence.

Looking to my left I noticed a handy bush and reached my hand out for it to hold onto as I guided myself off the path, but then I fell flat on my face. The bush was merely another trick of my mind, which was currently fucked up beyond all repair.

Laid out on the ground, the cold earth and dried grass pressed hard into my face, I gathered my last reserves of energy. I placed my hands by my sides and pushed myself up, pulled down my tights, and squatted.

What happened next is what I regard as being the lowest point in my life. Not in running, not in racing or traveling, but simply life in general.

I did my business, but as I was finishing my legs began to shake, no longer able to support my own weight. I was so weak that I just fell straight down into it. And I just laid there, I could not get up, I could not pull my tights on, I could not move. My vision began to flicker and coldness encompassed my entire body, freezing me to the core.

Sprawled out on the ground, barely off the trail with my tights around my knees, yaks and Nepalese men and women would occasionally walk by me. Some would keep moving, eyes straight ahead without giving a second glance towards me. Others would look down on me and shake their head before continuing to ignore my pathetic shape on the ground.

In all my life, I have never felt so close to actually dying. I'm still not sure if it was just the cold wind smacking against my half-naked body sprawled on the ground or if I could actually feel the life being drawn out of me.

After Ironman events and some of the longer ultra marathons, like in Patagonia, I thought I had known the feeling of exhaustion. Now it was clear that in those prior races I had felt nothing. Those races induced a mere fraction of fatigue compared to the utter and complete exhaustion that my body was now experiencing. Every muscle fiber in my body was beyond the point of function. Yet, cutting through to the small core of true awareness, a defining thought ran across my mind: I will not die while lying in my own shit.

Pressing my hands into the dirt, I counted to three and pushed myself very, very slowly up and off the ground. My head began to spin so I crouched back down and while doing so, pulled my tights back up over me. Even slower this time, I stood up as tall as I could, put my right foot forward, then my left, and kept on going.

After what seemed like forever, the Sherpas at the mile twenty-three checkpoint came into view down the bottom of the hill. I staggered up to the group of Nepalese and handed my running pack to the closest one so he could tie the red and white striped ribbon around my bag. Lying back down, the ground felt as comfortable as a bed in a luxury hotel room.

They stood over me and bantered back and forth in their native tongue. I was totally oblivious to the conversation the five or six people crowded over me were having.

"Cookie? Tea?" One of them finally said to me in English.

I shook my head, no, and muttered out, "I just need to rest for a bit."

My mind drifted and they continued to talk in Nepalese over me. A minute or two had gone by when one of them looked down at me, shook his head, and in plain English just said the single word, "Fucked."

That's it! My mind screamed. I immediately stood up, took my bag back and began to walk. Despite the dire state of my physical being, my pride remained, now more fired up than I had been in hours. It was just the spark I needed to get the train rolling again.

Huge mistake. I had only walked maybe ten steps before my body made its thoughts on that plan known. *Damn, I am exhausted. I just have to make it far enough to get around a corner so they can't see me, and I'll sit down again for another rest.*

Fifty feet later I felt like I was going to pass out and leaned against a rock wall to save myself from collapsing. Turning my head back towards the Sherpas I saw them all staring at me with wide eyes, unsure what to make of what had just transpired.

I just want this to be done. I never want to run again. I never want to travel again, I never want to move again. I just want to be home on the couch with a pint of Ben and Jerry's. Normally tuned into embracing the culture I was in, my mind attempted to console itself with the thought of any possible Western comfort.

At around twenty-four miles is where I first saw Tom moving up a hill towards me. He was headed out on his loop to the last Sherpa checkpoint with John and Daithi following closely behind him. Tom looked up to see me staggering down the trail moving this way and that with no coherent pattern to my movement.

"Hey, Bobby!" He yelled to me. "Stop messing around with us!"

I didn't reply to him, or at least I don't remember replying to him, and that's when he realized how much trouble I was actually in.

"Damn," he gasped out. "You stay here, and we'll come get you on the way back." His exact words to me are fuzzy and I barely remember the exchange, but that was the gist of it.

I mumbled something incomprehensible to him; he patted me on the back and kept going. As John and Daithi went by they too slapped my back and kept moving. My mind had not even registered what should have been the most important question: where's Frank? They were meant to be running the event as a team.

Still hallucinating, my perception and judgment clouded, I did not stay put, but continued to move forward along the trail. Other runners passed, but I said nothing, my head pointed down, my brain on a totally different planet.

I'm not sure how much time had gone by, but I was leaning with my face against a stone when the lads found me. Lights flickered in my brain and everything was beginning to feel deeply cold.

"Come on buddy," one of them said to me, and interlocked my arm with his. I looked up to see Daithi with a big stupid grin, smiling at me. "You aren't done with this race yet, brother. Not by a long shot."

Tom came under my right arm. "We're doing this together now."

John led the way and we stumbled our way along. For the next 1.5 miles I apologized to them, I thanked them, and I puked all over myself. Slowly but surely we made progress, fifty painful meters at a time. Small goals kept me motivated and the words of encouragement from my friends fueled me. Now dry heaving every few minutes, my body finding nothing left to reject, we continued on. This race was no longer about finishing my seven continents. The thought of that achievement had been relegated from my priorities several hours ago; this was now purely about surviving.

Organizing coherent speech, I said to the lads through parched lips, "Where's Frank?"

Tom shook his head. "He didn't make it. Sick as a dog back when we were running by the Pheriche checkpoint, what you have now knocked the crap out of him last night, he was starting behind the eight ball."

This glimpse of what could have been my fate played itself out in my mind's eye. The "what ifs" kill you, but it was a game that kept my mind occupied. Had I gotten it out of my system last night, I might have been fine and finished the race an hour ago. But on the other hand, I might have ended up like Frank.

This stimulus seemed to rejuvenate my mind to a slightly higher state of function, so I continued to stoke the fire as much as I could. I began doing math problems in my head. I converted things from imperial to metric and then back the other way, anything at all to keep the tenuous grip on reality I had mustered.

The lads told me jokes and stories, ribbing me for needing three old Irish dudes to save the young, strong American's "arse," to which I quickly corrected them to "ass."

We rounded the corner to see Namche Bazaar come into view. The familiar sight of the village lifted my heart and my legs. Then below us, we saw something none of us expected.

A larger figure was struggling up the hill, very late to be beginning the Thamo Loop, but moving steadily nonetheless. It was Frank.

"Frank!" John yelled. Frank raised his arm in acknowledgement and continued onward.

"Go," I said to the three of them. "Help Frank, I can make it in from here."

"Not a chance." They unanimously agreed. If Frank had made it this far after how debilitated he appeared fifteen miles ago, he was surely good to continue on his own now.

Guilt overwhelmed me. They were helping me, someone they had met a mere three weeks ago, as opposed to their old friend and countryman. I was too tired to argue. Frank looked strong, and he was, but now he had a long, lonely journey ahead of him as darkness began to engulf the valley.

We moved swiftly down the hill, the four of us covering the ground together as one unit, each step quicker as the finish line approached ever closer. Suddenly, our feet had left the dirt and we were once again on the cobblestone streets of Namche Bazaar.

People in the street stared and then clapped as the four of us passed by. The finish line now in sight, I removed my arms from the Irish grasp they had been supported by, and placed them instead over their shoulders. The four of us crossed the finish line as one, to the roar of our friends and spectators, some eight hours and twenty minutes after we started.

Everything was fuzzy after that. I recall a doctor ushering me inside, laying me down and covering me with blankets while he evaluated me. A few moments after, one of the Sherpas came in and placed the medal around my neck with a big smile on his face.

My head still pounded and I remained disoriented. It wasn't until a Scot named Stevie came in with seven fingers held high and in his broad accent proclaimed, "Ya did it, Bobby! Seven continents! Bloody well done!" that it finally dawned on me that I had completed my goal.

This wasn't the finish that I had imagined. The daydreaming and visualization that had gotten me through so many hard days was a million miles from the reality of how I completed my last continent. There was no glamour, no glowing, triumphant finish picture I could send home to my family and friends. There was a time when I would have felt true disappointment to have been deprived of this, the victorious movie ending to my story.

But instead there was a photo of four now lifelong friends, crossing the finish line together, exhausted and beaten, our faces beaming with pride and honor. A moment I will cherish forever, and a humbling end to my journey across seven continents.

Later on, we would wait outside to watch Frank cross the finish line as nighttime fell—the last and strongest finisher of them all.

On the long journey back to Kathmandu, as is typical for the region, our flights were canceled out of Lukla and we were deprived of normal civilization for yet another day.

We eventually made it back and had our last yellow team celebration together before going our separate ways, but we all knew we would meet again, especially Fiona and my Irish brothers, whom I now felt I owed the world to.

After a short flight to India and a nine-hour layover, I began to type this chapter. As a sixteen-hour direct flight to New York lay ahead of me, I reflected on the past two months. With pride, I grasped at my Everest Marathon medal tucked safely inside the breast pocket of my jacket. It was the final piece of my global puzzle. This trip, like the others before it, had changed me, teaching me through experiences about the world and the life that I want from it. It was the bookend of an adventure that was motivated by something I no longer really thought about. The bombing was my past and those demons no longer plagued me. I had succeeded in the physical quest but more importantly, I had come out the other side of an emotional journey, one which had brought me to a place of strength and peace.

No longer was I the seventeen year old signing up for my first marathon with my parents' credit card, and gone were the days where I chose a race because of a flashy jacket or a large crowd to cheer for me. The nightmares and terror that had plagued me for so long, limiting my life with their grip, were now absent. I was a new person; stronger, wiser, and richer than I could have ever imagined when I first set out on this mission. By no means was I financially rich (I was honestly flat broke after this last adventure), rather, I had gained friendships and memories that most people will go their whole life without ever knowing. If it hadn't have been for the worst day of my life, motivating me to leave my comfort zone and step outside the front door, I would have never experienced the best days of my time on this planet. So in many ways, the journey was far from over. Now I was ready to continue living the way life should be lived: freely, openly, and without fear.

EPILOGUE

Glenmore, Scotland
November 2018

I t was an incredibly difficult decision to decide to put my story in the form of a book. Frequently it was painful to recall many of these memories and translate them into words that would adequately portray my feelings, but it was important for me to record this for myself if not for anyone else, the reflection providing a sense of closure I had not yet achieved.

For my family and friends, I hope that this serves as a journal of sorts, bridging the gaps and delivering context behind my social media posts and frequent absences over the past few years. I've been away from home a lot, missing birthdays and holidays, celebrations and nights at the bar, so it is important for me to explain what this meant to me and why I needed to do it.

A major motivating factor for piecing together my travels was to hopefully inspire others who are struggling like I was, and sometimes

still am. Mental health problems such as PTSD can be silently debili-
tating, limiting life to an incredibly small radius. If I had chosen to back
down and be consumed by fear and sadness, I would never have had
any of the experiences that make this book, and ultimately make me.
I would live each day still controlled by the presence of past trauma,
prisoner to its powerful reach through time. Reading books of others'
adventures certainly inspired me and instilled the confidence that what
I was feeling and doing was indeed normal to an extent. Unfortunately,
I always felt somewhat disconnected when reading about my adventure
heroes because they appeared superhuman, but me—I'm a very average
guy when you break it down.

At the time of writing this I am twenty-five years old, paying off
a massive amount of student loans, and am still very unsure of what
direction I want my life to go. I'm not a professional runner, I'm not
incredibly fast, and companies aren't chomping at the bit to have me
wear their shoes...yet (Hi, Salomon!).

Although often thought to only be born from war zones, PTSD
is a condition that affects the lives of millions of people each and every
day. My way of handling it, believing I could do it myself by searching
for inner peace around the world, may not be for everyone. I very likely
should have sought professional help as well. Just as we would go to the
doctor to mend a broken arm, it is equally important to seek help if your
brain is the body part that is suffering. When I set out on my quest to
run on every continent, I thought the adventure would heal me, but it
was actually the people I met, conversations had, and lessons learned
from them that truly made the difference. Honestly, I believe the most
important way to manage this is through talking to someone, whether
it's professionally or just a good friend over coffee. Hiding the dark
thoughts and struggling on only led me to a very lonely and bleak place.

This story is born from a time when I felt my life was at its lowest
point. Fear weighed so heavily on me that I thought I could never enjoy
life again, never mind running. In those days, all hope was lost and

any solution seemed impossible or stupid. This is where the proverbial tipping point lives. It's when the light is furthest away, seemingly out of reach through an endless tunnel. It was at this stage that I took a step back and was able to see how much the grip of past events was possessing and controlling my everyday life, and I hated what I saw. I hated it enough to feel an energy that I was able to begin to turn to hope. This was now the perfect time to reset, rethink, and take a chance. I held my breath and closed my eyes tightly, put fear in the backseat, and took a leap.

It is so incredibly easy to put things off for another day, especially when you are crippled by fear, stress, anxiety, or a combination of all of these. I was incredibly lucky to have so many supportive people in my life, allowing me to feel comfortable enough to begin this adventure no matter how difficult or impossible it seemed at the start. I just needed the courage to take that first step. What I did was not conventional by any standard, and there have been some that have not been able to accept or understand the route I have chosen. Many people feel it is important to them to have a career or a family that defines their idea of success, and my achievements certainly do not fit easily into any of these categories. It has been freeing to realize that your life does not need to be clearly defined or on a single path at this, or any, age. I choose what's important because it's unique and specific to me. It doesn't have to be my neighbor's, friend's, or family's definitions, or what they want it to be for me. I hope that I will always have the strength to ensure my priorities are exactly what they need to be in that moment.

I had to be very creative to navigate the financial hurdles that stood in my way for the astonishing amount of expenses I incurred to travel as much as I did. I worked three jobs as a paramedic per-diem for sixty to seventy hours per week for three or four months, busting my ass because I knew an adventure was at the other end of it. When I had enough money in my bank account saved up, I would go and travel for as many months as I could. It was all about prioritizing what had become truly important in my life. I knew that I would rather have a full passport than a full bank account. I've regretted drinking too much, eating shady street food, and many of my choices on islands in Honduras, but I have never ever regretted going on an adventure. We aren't given enough time on this planet to see the whole world. But it would be a damn shame if we didn't use the time we have to see as much as we can. When we say things like "some day" or "maybe next year," the reality is that one day, there will be no tomorrow.

When I began to just book trips on this premise, seizing all the opportunities in front of me, I felt increasingly connected to the world, with more belief that certain things are just meant to be. Beginning this journey to run marathons, that was all it was; it was solely about the race. Over time, I came to the realization that out of a couple months abroad, the marathon lasted for only a few hours. Running was just the vessel that delivered me to all of these incredible experiences, and even more importantly to all the wonderful people that are now present in my life. Early on I learned that it's often the people, not the place, that dictate your experience. Just as Jo and I had the incredible experience at Wild in Chile, the people I met along the way made this journey special for me more so than the places themselves.

Conversely to the marathon bombing, Rachel's death still affects me deeply, more so than I could have imagined. My friend Parker Schenecker once said in a speech, "Whoever coined the phrase 'time heals all' didn't know me. It's more painful every single day." Some days I feel good, and others make it feel like it will never get any easier. The unanswered questions and lack of closure evoke a special kind of hurt, and one that I am still learning how to process and live with.

Aside from Rachel, I've been very fortunate not to experience the loss of those close to me. Frequently I am surrounded by death at work, but anyone in emergency medicine knows that the sorrow you feel tends to fade after a while. The repeated exposure eventually results in numbing of this response, a protective adaptation kindly carried out by your subconscious. It's a sad thing to admit, but it is true. With Rachel's passing I felt far from numb. I felt raw and I felt pain. Similar to Alex Sheen and his father, I knew I needed to remember Rachel for how she lived, and not how she died. My favorite memories of Rachel were not the ones made at work, but all the time we had spent together in the mountains. Just a few months after finishing the Everest Marathon, I went on another adventure to attempt to achieve that closure.

Rachel was one of my biggest supporters when it came to encouraging me to thru-hike the Appalachian Trail (AT), a hike in the eastern United States spanning roughly 2,190 miles from Georgia to Maine. It's an adventure of epic proportions that had often occupied my brain as a possibility, its presence increasing with relentless intensity since her death. So I took my own advice, told myself that one day there would be no tomorrow, and I went for it. If ever I felt unsure of my decision, I had only to draw upon all the encouragement present in the memories of my conversations with Rachel.

From April 11th to August 31st of 2018, I thru-hiked the AT for both of us. After 143 days in the woods, I summited Mount Katahdin on a crystal-clear day, and let Rachel experience one of the proudest moments of my life, through my eyes.

Now I can say that I feel healed from the tragic events that altered my life on April 15th, 2013. My long walk through the woods has gone some way to subdue the chronic pain I experience from Rachel's death. The pain hasn't completely gone, and I truthfully don't believe it ever will, but now there are more good days than bad. In all honesty the past four years have been quite successful if you use the measures that I do. I'm still not entirely certain where I want my life to go next, but maybe that's not a bad thing. I like to think that the day you stop asking questions and seeking answers is the day you lose your purpose.

I have discovered that I believe in fate and the concept that certain things happen to you in life when, and only when, they are supposed to. The circumstances of my life allowed for me to have the experiences that make up this book and that ultimately led me to growth and healing. For these to be available to me I had to take many other steps, both practically and emotionally, to ensure I was ready and open to opportunity. So often in a world of instant gratification we rush, hurry, take shortcuts, and become frustrated when the next stage in our journey is not clearly placed in front of us. We are all guilty of it. It is a part of how our society is structured and incentivized, but that cliché about the journey being more important than the destination, well, there's something to that. All you can do each and every day is make strides to become the best *you* that *you* can be, and trust that everything else will follow.

ACKNOWLEDGMENTS

Even though I have included this many times over the course of my story, I could never truly thank my parents, Lin and Bob, enough. Without them, I would have never had the courage to pursue any of my adventures. Their endless support and encouragement through the good times and bad have inspired me to chase my dreams. My mom and dad are the reasons that this story became a story at all.

My Nana B competes with my mom for being "my number one fan." Although I have been fortunate enough to have incredible adventures around the globe, I can honestly say some of my fondest memories are with her close to home. Being able to stay in touch with her while away and receiving her endless messages of support and joy is something I will treasure forever.

Jim Gagne is my role model and inspiration for any adventure I have ever dreamed of. Without his expert knowledge and guidance, I am sure I would have failed miserably in many of my endeavors. I am very lucky to call him a friend, and it is a true honor to know him.

John Lee became like a brother to me after his near-drowning when we were fifteen years old in the summer of 2009. Having no siblings of my own, John has been there for me in times when I felt like there was no one else. His advice and counsel throughout my life and in writing this book have been instrumental to any semblance of success.

Thank you to my cross country coach at Saint Anselm College, Paul Finn. His reassurance in the weeks, months, and years following the Boston Marathon bombing while I was away from my own parents at school comforted me in the times I felt most lost and alone.

Elinor Walsh, Tim Madigan, and Lucy Waite were instrumental in the multiple stages of editing this manuscript. Their incredible amount of dedication and hours spent combing over each and every word was invaluable to making this book worth reading.

Additionally, my group of friends from Saint Anselm College have been very supportive and understanding of me leaving for long periods of time and missing important gatherings (Fantasy Football drafts). It was not always the travel and adventure that cheered me up, more often than not it was the inevitable laughter and good times had with Brendan Mullin, Brian Higgins, John McNeil, Brendan McCormick, Kyle Beaulieu, Ashley St. Denis, Niles Harris, James Cassidy, Sierra Swords, Shannon Sholds, Erin Moreau, Ben Fox, and Jacob Plourde.

When I was far from home and my group of friends was nowhere near, all of my new companions that I met all over the world filled the large void. I've learned more than I could ever imagine from them and will feel forever indebted to the universe for placing them in my life.

Brad Newbury, John McNeil, John Lee, Fiona Smith, and Ryan Sandford have to be mentioned for their incredible patience and diligence in reading the early drafts of this book that were far from suitable to publish. Their unique perspectives helped me craft this into something I am proud of; I could not have gotten here without them.

ABOUT THE AUTHOR

Born in Boston, Massachusetts, Bobby O'Donnell spent his childhood in rural New England. A 2016 graduate of Saint Anselm College in Manchester, New Hampshire, he continues to work in emergency medicine as a paramedic when he's not traveling.